"*It's All in the Delivery* delivers powerful key principles that apply to our work and personal lives alike, namely exposing the very basic truth: it's all about the people. Keeping that one principle in mind will transform the way you evaluate situations, projects and personal challenges. Debi Brown shares her insight into the "people matter" principle with a set of prescriptive approaches to handling a challenge from initial engagement to successful outcome. This is a must-read if you want to improve your performance as well as the performance of your team."

—Ido Gileadi, partner, CAPCO

"*It's All in the Delivery* gives you insight into your ability to lead others in all things; a remarkable, prescient book."
—Mary Lucas, author of *Lunchmeat and Life Lessons: Sharing a Butcher's Wisdom*

Great Job On Your Journey to One!

Debi Brown.

It's All
in the
Delivery

It's All in the Delivery

Debi Brown

Clarity Advisory Services Inc.

For further information, please visit:
www.Itsallinthedelivery.ca

Printed in The United States of America

Library and Archives Canada Cataloguing in Publication

Brown, Debi, 1964-

It's All in the Delivery
How to Move Mountains Without Crushing the Villagers
Debi Brown.

ISBN 978-0-9812098-0-7

1. Leadership. I. Title.

HD57.7.B764 2009   658.4'092   C2009-901454-8

To my husband, Dennis,
who has always been there for me
and supported my career.
You are one of a kind and the love of my life!

To my children,
Cody, Chelsea and Scot
who have had to share me with my work family.
Thank You – I love you!

To my mom,
who taught me to never give up
and that I could do anything.
I know you are looking down at me with a smile!

To my teams,
who have been my inspiration
to be a better leader.
I learn every day from each of you – Thank You!

Contents

Acknowledgments

Writing this book has been an amazing experience and has been a several year project for me. I've received so much support from more people than I can list here but would especially like to thank: Danny Aleksic, Sandra Atri, Dragana Bajsanski, Peter and Blanche Bergin, Lucy Boetto, Daria Brown, Darlene Brown, Kelly Chan, Kelly Epperson, Gerry and Nicole Grennan, Sarah Groen, Cathy Fantauzzi, Esperanza Martinez and Laurie Simpson. All of you supported me in so many unique ways to complete this book and in addition, many of you spent an incredible amount of time helping me fine tune ideas and validate my thoughts. Thank You from the bottom of my heart!

In addition to all the people who helped me with the book,

there are so many leaders that I have been blessed to have worked with shoulder-to-shoulder over the years: Mary Rose Arnold, Vernon Barback, Ted Beaton, Pam Beauchamp, Neil Bisset, Lucy Boetto, Ian Camacho, Hilda Clanachan, Gerry Connolly, Armand D'accordo, Colette Delaney, Fred DiGiacinto, Kieran Ebbs, Phil Emond, Malcolm Eylott, Cathy Fantauzzi, Jonathan Fidgeon, Donal Finn, John Finigan, Chris Ford, Ido Gileadi, Linda Igra, Tony Kerrison, Ron Lalonde, Andy Leonard, Art Mannarn, David Marshall, Hugh Mcfadden, Tom Mcilwham, Michael Moerman, Daphne Myler, Michelle Neidermeyer, Margaret Shorten, Gilbert Swinkels, Mike Woeller, and Debby Young. You all were at my side through so many roles and projects over the years. I learned from each of you, and thank you all so much for the opportunity to have worked with you!

Foreword

I first met Debi Brown when I was working in London at a company that was struggling to bring an amicable but challenging merger with another firm to fruition. Project Knightsbridge, as the merger is referred to herein, was a complicated, multinational endeavor and an event that contributed significantly to the changing financial services landscape of the late 1990s. It serves as the foundational case study and a point of frequent reference in the pages that follow, as it was a project that seemed destined to fail—but one that was rescued and made successful using the principles that Debi outlines in the present work.

Despite the collective knowledge and best efforts of the

team assigned to Project Knightsbridge, we found ourselves at a loss as to how to deal with a rapidly closing ninety-seven-day window of time to sort out all the operational, regulatory and technology-related aspects of amalgamation. Frankly, we weren't sure if it could even be done. Then, Debi arrived on the scene. She immediately set about making changes—restructuring the project team to take advantage of each member's strengths, creating new ways to manage work and measure progress and applying infectious levels of enthusiasm to solving problems. In short order, the project team was reenergized and the merger brought back on track. She had found a way to motivate the team to achieve its goals against seemingly impossible odds.

Something in the way Debi approaches—or rather embraces—her tasks and leadership responsibilities brings out the best in the people around her. I can honestly say that the Herculean effort that the Knightsbridge team put forth to successfully meet our ninety-seven-day deadline was as much in response to the personal nature of requests from Debi as it was to the corporate targets on which we would ultimately be evaluated. I can still remember her asking for assistance in meeting project milestones with her hands clasped, pleading, "Please, please, please." With Debi as our leader, those of us working on Knightsbridge became more like a family than a project team. Making Knightsbridge a success became personal for us both individually and collectively.

Since Knightsbridge, I have had the good fortune to work with Debi on several initiatives. She continues to impress me with her ability to quickly earn the trust and respect of team members, tackle complicated issues and execute projects. Many colleagues over the years have similarly marveled at Debi's success as a project manager and leader of people. "How does she do it?" they ask.

We are fortunate that Debi has agreed to share her secrets for success with *It's All in the Delivery*. Using the approach she outlines in the following pages, you will become a better manager of people and, by extension, a more successful manager of projects. The timing of the publication of this book is auspicious for those of us who are charged with managing teams and projects during these troubling economic times. More than ever, organizations are trying to make important changes quickly, but with fewer resources. To be successful, we need to focus on people as much as tasks. The notion that people matter is at the heart of Debi's proven approach to successfully leading change, and it's a philosophy that I share.

I have learned that when you tackle a new project—be it an acquisition, a merger, a product launch, a restructuring or any of the multitude of other things you may become involved in—and you take the time to get to know the people on your team, you will be amazed at the synergies that develop and the success you can achieve. In other words, when you treat people like people and not cogs in a corporate wheel, when you value their experiences and opinions, and when you trust them, they will set petty politics and personal ambitions aside and put their energy into delivering results. Debi Brown has proven it time and again at different organizations and across different continents.

If you follow Debi's recipe for successfully delivering change, you too will be able to move mountains without crushing the villagers.

—Malcolm Eylott
Global head of Operations and Technology
TD Securities
April 2009

When I first decided to write this book, it wasn't because I wanted to "write a book." It was because I needed to say what so many of us long to believe: In today's fast-paced, crazy-busy, "I must be successful at all costs" kind of world, YOU CAN attain your goals and achieve your desired results while maintaining a number one principle—PEOPLE MATTER!

If you are like me, you strive to ensure that the people you interact with on a daily basis, whether they are colleagues or friends, know that their contributions and opinions are important.

My experience in both project management and executive-level management has shown me time and time again that if we fail to illustrate to others that they matter and that they are valued, everything we attempt to accomplish will be more difficult and less fulfilling.

Every day we must deliver results, regardless of our profession or vocation, and how we deliver those results makes a difference in our level of personal and professional success. Delivering results can also be very difficult when faced with incredibly challenging situations, and as the stakes get higher, we sometimes struggle with how to keep our wits about us and sustain our approach of even and fair-handed leadership.

I maintain that no matter the challenge or the delivery goal, it is always best to get right back to the basics. The same skills that help a fifth-grade teacher manage a school play to successful completion are actually the same skills that help me deliver a multi-million-dollar project to completion, all with successful results.

Over the years, I've built up a toolkit that has helped me tremendously when working with teams on challenging projects and initiatives. I'd like to share those tools with you. These tools will help guide you in incorporating a people-first priority into your day-to-day activities. The rewards will not only be for you and the people you work with, but also for those that you live with and play with.

My goal is that this toolkit will help you DELIVER RESULTS through building HIGH-PERFORMING TEAMS while following the KEY PRINCIPLE that PEOPLE MATTER! In this way, you and your teams will deliver the promised results and, during the process, no one will get crushed!

I have been asked over and over again to put the management and leadership concepts that I use into book form, so here it is. My expertise is in the banking industry, but these principles apply to every person in all careers and projects. Believe me when I tell you: You Can Do Anything… It's All in the Delivery!

Thanks for reading.

Chapter 1

Delivering Results With People in Mind

I can still taste those mashed potatoes. It's been over ten years, but they were the best that I have ever eaten, and that moment in London is forever lodged in my memory. Not just because of the food, but because of the thoughts that were forming in my head over that dinner.

"Do you guys trust me?" I asked. I was young, female, and Canadian. I had only been with this new firm for less than six months and worked out of our New York office. My two colleagues looked at me with anticipation.

The project was a merger and our lead London executive who was running the operation had to leave due to a personal emergency. My two colleagues were already there on the ground, trying to get a grasp of the situation, as there had been several problems facing the team. This was a project in crisis.

I had been working out of my office in New York City when I got the call to go help sort out the problems in London. Sparing you the nitty-gritty details, I will only say that with mergers, time is the key factor. The team needed me to get there, and get me there very quickly. Back then, the Concorde was the only way to make that happen.

I drove back from New York City to our home in Connecticut to quickly pack an overnight bag, and jotted a hurried note for my husband, who was out with the kids. Then in a blur, I was on the Concorde. When I landed, I wondered what was waiting for me, and I also felt terribly guilty about how I'd left my family behind.

I called my husband from London. "Hi, honey. I won't be coming home tonight. I'm in England."

Dennis, my rock, took it in stride. We both assumed I'd be home late the next day. And what is the golden rule with that word "assume"? Don't do it. Never assume anything.

The second call home was to explain that I needed a few more days in London. I was getting a handle on the crisis, but I just needed a little more time. I thought maybe things were coming together, and I could be on my way back home.

The third call to Dennis was, "Honey, can you and the kids come visit me in England?"

I went home ninety-seven days later.

SO WHY IS THIS STORY SO IMPORTANT?

We all have some technical training in our chosen field, whether formal or informal. My technical training has been in technology and operations for the banking industry, as well as project management. I've held junior positions and executive positions, been a staff member and a consultant. In all roles, it is clear that the technical training was key as a basis for success, but it doesn't get the job done entirely.

There are many existing books that will help any of us improve our technical or business skills. This book is meant to serve as an additional reference tool. Rather than focus in these pages on the "what" in our everyday work, I would like to focus on the "how."

I've proven to myself time and time again that what I noticed early on in my career continues to be the key to my success—the principle that I mentioned in the very beginning: People matter. You'll be hearing me say those two words a lot.

I was very aware in the beginning of my career that too many executives readily sacrificed their teams to achieve their own personal career goals. The people that these leaders worked with seemed to be nothing more to them than workhorses to use and abuse and forget about when the project was completed. Their attitude and work mentality was the exact opposite of "people matter." It appeared that for many managers, the people on their teams did not matter at all.

I couldn't believe that was how one truly succeeded and if it was, I couldn't be a part of it.

Now some twenty-years down the road, I'm here to tell you that their way is not the only way to achieve success. In my eyes, their way is not success at all.

The project that I started to tell you about in the mashed potatoes story, the London merger, was almost exactly at the end of my first ten years in this field and the beginning of my next. Since the time this London merger mission was achieved, I've gone on to many other personal, community, and professional challenges.

The fundamental principles that I adopted early in my career were completely exercised in London and proved to me that success does not have to come at the cost of others. I now apply these basic tenets to all of my undertakings, and they have been proven over and over and over again to work ever since.

You could call the London merger project a light bulb moment, the defining moment, or my a-ha moment. Call it whatever you want. I simply and profoundly knew that my gut and my head agreed, and that my approach of building teams and getting things done was right. I also knew that my approach could work no matter what the project scope or timeframe. With this particular project, the stakes were very high and the timeline very short, which was the catalyst for me questioning everything I had believed!

DELIVERY STARTS WITH YOU

My job is all about delivering results, and if you are reading this book, then yours is, too. You can deliver the goals or the goods as expected, and while meeting those goals, all people involved can be treated with dignity and respect, and everyone involved can be motivated to deliver. That's a tall order and yet it is possible! Treating all people right does not come at the cost of a late or shoddy delivery. You do not have to sacrifice one element to achieve the other.

I understand that getting things done in a delivery-focused world can add stress to peoples' lives. Yet, acquiring the leadership skills and the ability to bring people together makes succeeding at delivery that much easier.

Some people come by it authentically; others have to acquire it. Dealing with people and with issues can get complicated, I know. That is the purpose and goal of this book and my "toolkit" that I will share with you.

I'm often asked, "Debi, how do you do it?"

The real question is: How do WE do it?

When anyone tackles a new project, most people usually first look at the deadline and think, "How can we make this happen in this short amount of time?" Time is always a critical factor, but the bottom line, the thread of it all, is the people. The focus—always, always, always—needs to be on the people. That element is what I think we have gotten away from over the years.

The corporate world can often be cutthroat, full of competition and people only looking out for themselves. I've seen it firsthand. However, that way is NOT the only way. I've put together this book after many years of working with amazing leaders and teams in a delivery-focused world, and I'm here to tell you that stomping on and crushing people is not the way.

All the thoughts and ideas that I have developed through many years of experience are in these pages, parceled into five key steps, which you will find critical to managing any project or initiative.

The FIVE KEY STEPS are:

1. **Embrace the Challenge**
2. **Form the Winning Team**
3. **Be the Leader**
4. **Stock up on the Soft Skills**
5. **Make It Happen**

The purpose of this book is to equip you to face the challenges of leadership and to feel prepared and confident. One of the most basic ways to get prepared is to have a toolkit that you can refer back to whenever you need it. With each step, I will provide tools to add to your personal toolkit. The five sets of tools aligned to each step in delivery are listed below:

1. **Embrace the Challenge Using the 3 Cs**
2. **Form the Winning Team With DEUCES**
3. **Be the Leader by Mastering the Art of Leadership**
4. **Stock up on the Soft Skills With the 4 Ls**
5. **Make It Happen With a Secret Formula**

When faced with a new situation or circumstance, you can review your toolkit much like your personal instruction manual and find what you need to carry on with the project. In any trade, there are technical guidelines and professional methodologies. Consider this toolkit a way to support a new methodology on HOW to get things done.

My goal is that at the end of this book you will have another methodology to use in the workplace, in addition to other training you have acquired.

Delivery Leadership: It's All in the Delivery

In addition to providing you with the steps required for a solid delivery approach and the toolkit to help you apply the approach in a practical way, I will also refer back to the London merger in each chapter under "Back to Delivery." I will use this merger as my backdrop for illustrating how some of my experiences validated the approach, along with some other more well known examples, such as the movie Apollo 13.

I want to use the merger as an example because it was a project that somehow had every possible problem and challenge associated with it. I could not make up a better fictional example to illustrate my points. This real "case study" is perfect. Because I can't use the real name of the project, I've given it a nickname, Project Knightsbridge. Knightsbridge is the area where I lived while in London. Or, I should say, I didn't really live there; we lived at the office, but I did grab a few quick moments of sleep here and there in Knightsbridge.

IT TAKES A VILLAGE TO MOVE A MOUNTAIN

Before we begin to walk through each step that is required for anyone to deliver results successfully, we must first agree on the FOUNDATIONAL PRINCIPLE that PEOPLE MATTER. We all know it takes a village to raise a child. Well, it also takes a village to get things done in the workplace and I refer to this village as our HIGH-PERFORMING TEAM.

Building and leading high-performing teams requires focus and commitment, and learning how to do this well is the key to achieving personal and professional success.

In addition to the time constraints in today's business world, there are also many other challenges that make it even harder for today's leaders to make things personal, and to apply their technical or operational training with real-life principles to lead teams to success. Today's leaders also have to complete big things in a small amount of time. This puts them in a very difficult position because it takes time to personally address how to mobilize and motivate a truly dynamic team, which is not easy to accomplish while rushing to meet a deadline.

In very simple terms, the village that needs to be mobilized today is built up of many different individuals from different training and backgrounds, and they need to join forces to deliver something that is sometimes new and challenging for them. Add to the mix the fact that they likely have not worked together for very long. Creating a high-performing team is not done in the blink of an eye and it is not a simple task.

In the history of the business world, teams were always department teams that had worked together for years and got to know each other over a long time. Today, we often need temporary teams to accomplish our objectives. This creates a challenge, but a challenge that can be made easier for all leaders who recognize that the "people matter" philosophy is the foundation for successful delivery. The foundation is not the timeframe. The foundation is not the delivery of results. The foundation is the people, and having that belief will translate into delivering results in the desired timeframe.

IT IS A MATTER OF TRUST

Projects today happen in a tight time period. There are no longer years to build the loyalty and trust among people who need to form a high-performing team. Loyalty and trust are two key ingredients that are essential for leaders to establish—and that now must be established very quickly—in order to enable the development of the high-performing teams needed to meet the delivery commitments.

It's well understood that relationships are built on trust. My family trusted that it was the right thing for me to stay those ninety-seven days in London. My colleagues placed their trust in me as well. That's why they had asked me to jet across the pond. The team on that merger project also learned to trust me, the new kid on the block. And I trusted in my abilities, and that it was the right thing for me to stay on.

I'll finish the mashed potatoes story and tell you about Project Knightsbridge as we go. At this moment (with no mashed potatoes in my mouth), I want to tell you that writing a book has taken me out of my comfort zone, but I also trust that it's the right thing for me to do. Ah, that word again: "trust."

In my banking industry business world, my reputation is somewhat established, but you may not know my reputation or have ever heard of me. Team members tell me that on a "Debi Brown team," they feel that they are truly cared for and that they know the direction of the team, the mission that faces them, and how to get to the end game even through tough times. They join the team knowing they will succeed.

On a high-performing team, the leader has to be the leader, but also the protector. So often, we do not see that in today's managers. I've known too many leaders who only protect one person—themselves—and let the team be the scapegoat. In my view, the leader is the one person who has to be willing to stand up and take the heat, as well as the person trusted to have the courage to make the decisions needed. Are you that person? Do you want to be that person?

My career has evolved in such a way that I find myself increasingly rescuing troubled projects. Things are usually pretty messed up and there is panic all around, with concerns about how everything will get done on time. When I am called in to take over and calm the storm, people continually ask me how I do it. How do I come in, regroup, and lead the team to the delivery?

To me, it is so simple—get in, get involved, and exhibit behaviors that create trust and lead to loyalty. I use these ingredients to create and sustain a high-performing team. When I look around, I see that this very basic concept is being overlooked. I want to scream it from the rooftops. If you treat people well, and form winning teams with that as your premise, you can achieve anything. Anything!

I wish I could stop there, or, in fact, I wish I did not have to write this book, but from what I have seen, many people do not see the connection. They concentrate only on the business aspects of a mission or project instead of getting to know the people on the team. It is my experience that by learning about the team members and getting to know each one a little bit better and utilizing them to the best of their ability, the team is able to achieve even more amazing results.

The key to any success I have had is that I have taken the time to learn the dynamics of the people on that project, and the number one priority that I hold dear is often what many managers fail to realize: People matter! (No, I will never tire of saying it.)

WHEN PEOPLE MATTER, THEY DELIVER!

We are all human beings and need to relate to each other as such. I know it seems like a given, doesn't it? However, I am continually amazed that with every new venture I become involved in, I have to tackle this issue.

Many managers today are not treating their teams with the dignity and respect that they all deserve, and what some don't yet understand is that this is not just about "soft skills" or "HR management." Getting things done requires energy and focus at all levels. Just like you would treat your body with respect if you were an Olympian, you must treat your team with respect if you wish to achieve Olympian-like results in the mission you are tackling.

In an age where reality television tells our youth that it is "all about me" or life is a competition and you must be the last man standing, I have to express my deep concern.

You can be ambitious, be a doer, and still be looking out for your team. No matter what line of work you are in, you have to produce an end result. You can be respectful of the team members along the way, but if you don't deliver, you won't stay employed— and if it's your company, you won't stay in business. It is what you do and how you do it that makes a difference. I may be repetitious in my motto that people matter, but if I didn't also get results with that motto, I would not even contemplate writing this book.

On Project Knightsbridge, one of the stakeholders gave me the nickname "the Canadian firecracker." I was there to get the job done, no doubt about it. Getting the work done and forging a group of individuals into a smooth-running team is my passion. I like to think that the "Canadian firecracker" term implies that I had positive energy and used it to spark them on to success, a group success.

My personal view on the need for trust and loyalty among team members has always been present in my leadership style. However, early in my career, I felt that by trusting and being loyal, I would just merely help make my job more pleasant. After taking on many different types of roles, including executive management as well as project management, I now see these leadership principles as the main reason that I have been able to guide teams to the desired outcome, so I view these attributes as a gift.

The world needs more people to realize that they, too, can be liked and respected as leaders and that it's okay to use their gifts as well. In fact, it's much needed.

I see that as a society we are all coming to the realization that working on our personal strengths and weaknesses leads to a longer life. We spend millions of dollars on self-improvement books and tapes. We strive to improve our communities, our families and even the environment. It's now time to take the mission of improvement into the workplace.

Whether such leadership values come naturally to you or require some effort, your workplace needs you to be your best and to ignite others to be theirs.

MAKING IT HAPPEN

Many project teams or departments that I have been invited to work with are in crisis mode involving "no way in hell is this gonna get done" kinds of situations. And every time, an amazing team that I've been so lucky to work with pulls it off.

The secret to managing a crisis project or challenging initiative is to mentor and direct the team on a daily basis to work with each other, all in order to ready them for the "go live" moment. But I am getting ahead of myself. I have many specific tactics to share along with real-life scenarios that will help put my advice into perspective. This book is meant to be a source of reference, a reminder for you when you need it, now and down the road, that it is possible to deliver against all odds.

The goal is that when you finish reading, you will believe in yourself and your ability to lead. Maybe you don't see yourself as a leader right now, or maybe you do and you just want more ideas to hone your skills. You will get practical advice here and how to apply it.

My tricks of the trade are not just for the trade. They are for all aspects of life. No matter what you are doing, in business, in family life, or in the community, everything is about directing individuals to work through thick and thin...together.

Anyone can simply get a job done. It is what a person does and how a person does it that sets him or her apart as a leader. When people ask, "How do you do it?" it should be because they see that the product is delivered, whatever that product may be, and that all the people who have worked tirelessly on the project feel good about it, they feel good about each other, and they feel good about themselves. The mountain was indeed moved and no one was crushed in the process.

You and your colleagues can get it (your particular project, your own "it") accomplished against all odds. Seemingly insurmountable challenges can indeed be conquered. There are several types of "get it done" missions in the workplace and at home. For this book, I've chosen to focus on projects as a way to deliver my message, but these toolkits can be used for all layers of leadership for all types of initiatives.

There's a positive current of energy that a good leader brings to his or her team in the face of any challenge, and as we all know, projects can create challenges on a daily basis. Successful managers are able to harness the energy and transform it into positive energy, for the good of the whole team and the ultimate benefit of the project.

Are you ready to tap into that energy? Are you ready to take a hard look at yourself, at your strengths and weaknesses? Are you ready to move that mountain?

We can. Step by step, we can do anything. So let's get started.

Chapter 2

STEP ONE: Embrace the Challenge

In this book, I've constructed an approach for DELIVERY that provides you with a methodology for "how" to achieve success all while keeping in mind the key principle: PEOPLE MATTER. Embrace the Challenge is the first of these steps that you need to adopt, and then customize, to fulfill your leadership goals to accomplish ANY delivery challenge.

1. **Embrace the Challenge**
2. **Form the Winning Team**
3. **Be the Leader**
4. **Stock up on the Soft Skills**
5. **Make It Happen**

This first step, embracing the challenge, may be easy to bypass, but it is very dangerous if you think that you can just skip it. You need to think through this step carefully.

We all know that before anything we do, to be done right, we must be fully committed and ready for the challenge. In project management, it is no different. As the leader, you are signing up for yourself, as well as the team you are about to lead, through what might be a rough and challenging mission. You must be ready for anything.

WHAT SHOULD YOU BE DOING FIRST?

The reason for embracing your challenge is to stop and think about your level of commitment, and also to ensure that anything your particular challenge forces you to deal with—obstacles, hurdles, crises—you will be able to handle. If you enter into the project fully embracing the challenge that lies before you, then you will ALWAYS SUCCEED, even when you have moments of failure, set back, or distress.

You must first take a moment to reflect on what success is and what it means to you. Sure, we all want to succeed, but what does that really mean? Succeed at what? If climbing up the corporate ladder is the only bulls-eye that you are shooting for, I suggest that you broaden your target. I want to dispel the notion that the top rung is all that matters. A ladder with only one rung is useless.

If I could, I would get rid of the whole corporate ladder imagery. I prefer a new mindset. My approach encompasses more than the corporate world. Applying the concepts in these upcoming chapters can certainly affect your work life, and improve it, and can also improve every area of your life. If you want to stick with a ladder mentality, view it as your *personal* ladder instead. This simple change in outlook has a profound impact. Your whole life will improve, including your life at work.

Most of us spend a lot of hours at our jobs. In managing delivery for any project or initiative, we tend to spend more hours at work than we do at home. Shouldn't we be able to enjoy those hours? I sure think so. I want you to want to spend those hours there motivating others to deliver results, to enjoy their work, and to work with others to achieve the mission that they have been asked to meet.

I love what I do, but there was an internal jolt when it hit me. Maybe even an external, physical startle reflex. I doubt a light bulb physically appeared over my head, but the dawn of realization settled over me. I realized that people were relying on me to make decisions, to steer the course through the rough and unknown waters that lay ahead, and they looked to me to be their guide. I had to dive in and embrace the challenge.

Your job as a leader is what should enter your mind while thinking about embracing the challenge. Your level of commitment to the team and how you accept the challenge will at some point play a key role in your ability to succeed, especially when times are difficult and things are not always going your way. The toolkit assigned to this step outlines how to do just that.

ADD TO YOUR LEADERSHIP TOOLKIT:

There are five steps in building your APPROACH TO DELIVERY, and to support them, there are five sets of tools to add to your toolkit. With this first step, Embrace the Challenge, the addition to your toolkit is the 3 Cs.

1. **Embrace the Challenge Using the 3 Cs**
2. **Form the Winning Team With DEUCES**
3. **Be the Leader by Mastering the Art of Leadership**
4. **Stock up on the Soft Skills with the 4 Ls**
5. **Make It Happen With a Secret Formula**

THE 3 CS

First things first...commit, connect and care. Whether the mission is large or small, it still doesn't matter. The focus on the team is the same. You must be in the game, you must connect with everyone involved, and you must care about the mission and the people.

COMMIT—"I'M IN!"

When you apply and accept a new leadership role, what goes

through your mind? If it is ANY of the following, then stop right now.

1. Great salary and benefits!
2. Fits perfectly on my strategy to climb the corporate ladder!
3. I'm going to be a hero at work if I get this done!
4. I'm so excited for my friends and my family to see how far I've come!

These are the WRONG reasons to get involved in a mission that has you leading others to succeed.

If you were to commit to leadership and delivering results because of any of the four goals that are listed above, when times get rocky (and they will), or when people get in trouble on the team, then your agenda will always be to meet the four "it's all about me" objectives above. You will not do what is really *right*. You will not be thinking about the team or the project or the delivery. You will be thinking about you, and that does not lead to success.

You might be able to pull off one project with those attitudes, but in the long run, you will not be able to deliver successfully and consistently if you have the "all about me" approach.

An important recognition is required on your part before you evaluate why you are taking on something challenging.

For some people, instead of the "all about me" attitude, they have the "I doubt me" complex. This, too, is common. Whenever new adventures are in front of you, there must be the realization that there will be a moment (the minute or hours after you sign up) when you think that you may be in over your head. That's natural.

As a matter of fact, any person who encounters a new challenge immediately faces the realization that they may not know everything about what they are about to do. This realization can lower your confidence and lead you to question your abilities. As a leader, you must be ready for this moment of doubt or fear. It's 100 percent normal. It does not mean that you are not up for the challenge.

However, if you have signed up to the challenge or the project for the wrong reasons, then you probably will ignore this dive in confidence and only concentrate on your self-serving goals. The fact that you do not experience this self-realization means that the very process of understanding how to achieve the mission will be missed. I would predict that you will eventually be sorry for this as you face and work through your inevitable challenges.

If you commit to a project based on the RIGHT five reasons, then you will find that you will succeed more often because your mindset will be right. When asked to take the reins for any project, as big and scary as it may be, these are the thoughts you should consider:

1. I believe in the goal the team has been given.
2. I believe my skills will help deliver results.
3. I don't have all the answers, but I will endeavor to find them in partnership with my team.
4. I know this opportunity presents me with new challenges but I am not too shy to ask for help.
5. I can visualize leading the team to the finish line.

Do you think that it sounds too Pollyanna-ish? I don't think so. Not at all. These thoughts are better than the self-serving attitudes mentioned before. No one has all the answers. A great leader knows how to surround himself or herself with the right people.

Actually, as a Canadian, I thought it was interesting to watch the American presidential election, and President Barack Obama's choices for key leadership positions. For example, I looked at his choice of Hilary Clinton for the role of secretary of state, and her responses to the challenge of this role.

The people associated with Hilary's team stated that this role was definitely not being accepted simply because it improves Hilary's résumé. People close to Hilary say that she accepted this position because she believes that at this time in the world, the mission for the secretary of state is critical for our future and that she believes her skills can help the country succeed in these challenging times.

A-ha...She answered the first two questions right and I'm very relieved. It's nice to know that the next U.S. administration is taking on roles and challenges for the right reasons. I believe that the team being put forward not only meets my first four criteria in the appropriate way for success, but that the parties involved really and truly believe in visualizing the finish line.

In politics, there really isn't an overall finish line, but there are specific goals and objectives that each one of them will be instrumental in achieving. From the outside looking in, I feel that these people are committed to the vision along with President Obama.

I'm sure they all know that their résumés will be better-looking at the end of their terms and that their egos played a part in their decisions. However, when weighing that perk against the risk of the current economy and the number of challenges facing them, at the end of the day, I do believe as human beings they made a decision based on the passion to change things and not the passion to only achieve career success.

It is my impression that they have a "team first/project first" mentality, and not a "me first" attitude. That is the key to success.

In the normal working world, you or I signing up for something should be no different. Bury your ego and the "me first" mentality. Commit to the mission. Committing to a new challenge and to a new team is critical and can be even more exhilarating when you sign up for something that you can visualize. Seeing the end goal keeps the fire in your belly going, instead of the calculated achievements that you may find that are in your head. The belly always wins! Commit to your missions and enjoy!

CONNECT WITH THE CHALLENGE AND THE TEAM

So let's stay with the village analogy for the moment. What if you were back in the times when you needed to be able to rally the villagers to face a battle? Or you had to convince them that all was well when they were all unsure that they could trust you? Or what would you do if they were even in a state of panic?

You'd need to convince them that all will be okay. You would definitely not be able to connect with them and their thinking if you did not know what was in their hearts. How do you learn that? Take the time and effort to connect with them.

You need to know about the people, about how their culture works, how they work as a team, what makes them comfortable, excitable, and unstoppable. Then and only then will you be able to truly lead them into battle and have any chance for success.

With a project, it is exactly the same. You've signed up…another deep breath or two to face the challenges ahead…and you are IN! Now, you need to connect with the team.

Connecting with the mission in front of you is also critical. The two are intertwined.

In most cases, when you take on something new, a team is ready and waiting for you. Very rarely are we stepping into something with no one on the team to begin the journey. If, however, you are entering a project where there is absolutely no current team, then this section is more about connecting with the individuals who understand the mission that you have been asked to take on.

Please also keep in mind that these stages of embracing the challenge are not always in order, and are not a one-time thing. There are many times when you will be in the middle of a project and need to go back to this step to reassess the strategy or to make right on some issues. You may also find that the "commit, connect and care" mindset is helpful in everyday leadership; for example, connecting with your team on a daily basis in a troubled project can provide the team with your energy injection at all levels at all times! We stay connected with our friends and family members. Our team members need the same commitment to connect with us as well.

Connecting with your team and understanding the mission

in front of you go hand in hand. The way to connect with your team is as easy to remember as A, B, C.

- ✓ **A**sk the team
- ✓ **B**e with the team
- ✓ **C**ommunicate with the team

Ask the Team

I'm sure that we have all said at some time in our careers, "Why does management look to outside experts and consultants to tell them what we, the people, already know!" Well, as leaders, we should remember that, and FIRST ask our team what they think and how they would advise us on options for completing the project successfully. I'm not saying that you won't need to still reach out for specialized external expertise, but it should not be your first option.

The first thing a new leader should do is sit with every team member possible and talk. If the team is ten people, have a sit-down chat with all ten. If the team is large, then you need to discover who the cultural leaders are and sit with them. To do this, pull all of the team together for a town hall meeting or strategy session. As questions are asked, you will begin to see which members of the team are the most vocal and if all other team members are looking at them when they speak instead of looking away. This is a clear sign that the person is viewed as a leader of the people.

Another approach I've used with teams that number in the hundreds is to have groups of thirty to fifty meet either in person or by phone. I invite them based on alphabetical order, that way I get a real mix across the organization or project. I then talk to them about who I am, why I'm there, and what the mission is. I specifically go into the session with pointed questions and then take the time to randomly pick out people to provide me with their general thoughts. This generates conversation and again, inevitably, the cultural leaders will stand out.

Either way, you must talk to the team and ask them about their views and how they see the situation. All individuals on the team must feel that you are engaged and that you want them to be engaged as well. There are many approaches to asking questions to get feedback; find your own and go with it, but do not let the size of the team intimidate you. You MUST ask the people what they see, what they think and how they view the mission!

On Project Knightsbridge, I remember that during one of the first team meetings, there was one particular individual, Riley, who spoke up. She openly asked questions and raised suggestions that clearly were on everyone's mind. I saw immediately that Riley would be a valuable member of the leadership team and I could see that the rest of the team trusted her. Asking the team doesn't only give you answers; it gives you insight into the existing culture and the cultural leaders as well. Riley and I are still good friends today and have worked on many "in trouble" projects together. Riley taught me early on that asking questions and openly discussing problems was the fastest and most powerful way to connect with a team!

Be With the Team

Yes, you are the leader, but you are not a one-person team. Don't just jump right in and expect that you have all the answers. After you have asked the team members about what they know and think, join in on their work to get comfortable with how they work and, more specifically, understand the content. It is extremely important to work with them and not above them.

One of the quickest ways to get up to speed on the work if it is already in progress is to take a look at the latest issues list or action items for the team. Read through and find the ones that are either the largest problems or the longest outstanding.

Ask the individual who is the primary person for the item to organize a work session on the item with the key people involved. Make sure they don't work all night to prepare a presentation; you need to get their true feelings on the issue, not a prepared status. Sit in front of a white board with them and have them teach you, and then work together to understand the active work around the item. Be with them on the discussion, not above them. Make it clear that you are eager and willing to understand their challenges and their work.

Another way to get up to speed quickly on the project and the team dynamics is if there is an activity that is in progress as you arrive on the scene. Simply be a part of the team, making them comfortable with your presence, and let them teach you what they are doing and see where you can help. Make sure it is always helping and not intimidating.

Your team members must trust that you are willing to roll

up your sleeves and work side by side on the details, and not just sit up top and take all the glory when times are good and blame them when times are bad. When I first arrived on the scene during Project Knightsbridge, one key executive named Elliot watched me closely and was a bit skeptical that I would actually make a difference. Elliot later told me these early thoughts of his and that once he witnessed me actually rolling up my sleeves to get to the bottom of the problems, he then realized I was here for the right reasons. He saw that I was willing to work side by side with the team to deliver the much needed results. When you work beside your team, you learn from them, they learn from you, and you become part of the work at its purest level.

Being with the team as you get up to speed is great for validating the strategy for the project as well. Take the project goals and objectives and review them in a work session with the individuals that will be leading your sub-teams. Make sure that they all have a part of the design stage for the project approach and that their feedback is well received and not easily written off. They are your team now and they will generate the energy for success, so do not leave them on the sidelines during the creation stages. They need to be a true part of the strategy. You need to be a true part of the operations.

Communicate Strategy With the Team

Now that you have ASKED the team members for their input, and you have BEEN a part of the team, you now need to integrate the best of all their thinking and complete your vision for how you need to lead them to deliver the project. You need to COMMUNICATE with the team.

Communicating the integrated thinking back to the team members lets the team as a whole know that they have contributed to your vision. The team also feels part of a unified approach immediately and they join in the ownership of the project. You would be amazed how many leaders come in and ask questions and then never reiterate back what they heard or how it impacted their vision or plans.

Your bar is high for your team, so expect the same from yourself. Transparency cannot be underestimated. It will be the basis for trust and communication.

Relationships (work and personal) are based on give and take. If you take the expertise and the efforts of the team members, you must also give them feedback. You must give them respect. That is the underlying facet of creating a connection with a team. You will be working with your team through some potentially difficult times so it is best to build the foundation properly from the beginning.

You confirm your trust and confidence in, and respect for, your team by communicating the project strategy with them. People want to know what they are doing and why they are doing it. Taking the time to communicate is the best time you can spend with your team.

A crucial aspect in any kind of relationship is communication. It's a make or break kind of thing. And why do we communicate with each other? We communicate because we care.

Connecting Through ABCs Every Day

A friend of mine was asked to take on a new team that was working in a warehouse in product distribution. Patrick was approached by the executives of a national firm to turn the productivity of this location around. He embraced the challenge and took on the position of the team's new executive leader. What was interesting about his story was that his approach followed the ABCs to a T.

On the first day, Patrick went in and walked around and talked with people. Then on the second day, and each day after that, he did exactly the same thing. Patrick showed interest in the work, the people, and the issues. Six months after religiously *A*sking the team, *B*eing with the team, and *C*ommunicating with the team, the executives called Patrick downtown for a meeting. He was also asked to bring the wage sheets with him. How curious!

When Patrick arrived downtown, he was told that the location he was running had previously been in last place for productivity and morale when compared to all the locations nationally. Funny thing—since Patrick took on his new role, at six months into his leadership, this location was now number one for productivity and morale.

The company executives wanted to know if Patrick had somehow managed to turn this team around with wage increases, as they couldn't possibly see any other way that it could have been accomplished. Boy, were they surprised at his response.

He explained to them the simple things that he had done. He started on day one, asked the team what they thought, spent each day being with the team to understand their jobs and their issues, and then responded to their needs wherever he could. Some issues had been easily remedied. The employees wanted windows that opened and picnic tables outside the warehouse to have lunch. Most importantly, they wanted to be heard. For many of us, it is a common sense approach, but in the corporate world, common sense can get lost in the fray sometimes.

Patrick wasn't always able to give them everything they were looking for, but he listened and he was with them. That's all he did. He led the team from last place in the company to first place, and all with a basic approach: Following the ABCs!

CARE ABOUT THE TEAM AND MOVE MOUNTAINS

You must care. I can't say it any other way. You must care about the people on your team and care about the quality of service that you and they are providing. Caring takes extra time and must be authentic. Caring is not just a soft skill; it relates to caring enough and building a team that cares enough about the quality so that you will all work very hard to integrate everyone's detailed understanding of the work facing you.

For some folks, caring is a natural inborn trait. They have an innate "people person" gene. For others, exhibiting a caring attitude may feel stilted at first. You don't have to be a touchy-feely type. All personality types must care about their team; how they show it is a personality thing. The important thing is for leaders to care and for the team to realize that the leader cares.

In general, we train our leaders to look at the bottom line, and we fail to concentrate on the human element. Good leaders may be analytical and logical, but that does not mean that they are exempt from caring.

Caring is what took my friend's team from last place to first place in six short months and when I look back to the very early part of my career, caring is also what helped me find my way to success. When I think back to how I got started as a consultant, it all seems so crazy.

My husband, Dennis, and I had a small computer store. Times were tight and we were young and struggling. All we had was determination, perseverance, and a strong work ethic. (My husband is one of twelve children. He was raised to know the value of a dollar and the value of earning that dollar.)

A customer stopped in one day needing an inexpensive external hard drive compatible for his brand name computer; with all brand name companies, they like customers to use their brand and not the inexpensive, potentially incompatible types. This man had been told that what he wanted was impossible to get.

He was at his wit's end when he stopped in our place. I told him to leave it with me for twenty-four hours; I would make it happen. I spent all night searching, and called him the next day with a solution to his need. I had in fact found something that could work for him. He was surprised and impressed. He thanked me, and I thought that was the end of the story.

I had no way of knowing that that one encounter would propel me to where I am today. This man called a week later and asked if I had ever thought about consulting work. I had indeed filled in at my uncle's company when a staff member had gone on maternity leave. I loved consulting work. This customer who I had helped out set me up for an interview and I got the position.

That job led to the next and the next, including junior executive and then senior executive roles. I applied my caring to all customers; —the teams I ran were my customers—I worked for them! Years later, I would find myself in New York and then in London with Project Knightsbridge…and the rest, as they say, is history.

Caring is critical. I had cared about a customer's needs even though there was no profit in it for us, but funny enough, it has paid forward ever since. I have always practiced the "do it and do it well" philosophy. In essence, I guess it is because I care. (My motto is "Go for 150 percent and you might actually achieve 100 percent.")

I also believe that every person matters. For instance, the person who hired you for the job is not any more important than the person who does the heavy lifting on the team. The super-famous client is not more important than the not-famous client. Position in society or the workplace should never affect your attitude, your behavior, or your caring.

Caring is the way that your connection remains with the team. That is the bottom line.

BACK TO DELIVERY

Let's go back to that night at dinner in London. It's like a scene in a movie to me now. I just remember it so well: The dinner was filet mignon with the most incredible mashed potatoes…oh, yeah, I already told you about them at the beginning. Maybe I was just really hungry.

I had arrived in London and had spent almost five days straight working with my colleagues and our teams, trying to find a way for us to meet the challenge. We had reviewed every issue, sat with the team to hear their concerns, and worked tirelessly to understand the problems so that we could find a way to fix them and meet the objectives of the merger. The crazy part of it all was that the merger had to be completed very aggressively and there were only ninety-seven days left to the target "go live" date.

We knew that the merger was critical to the strategy of the company overall and we knew that failure was not an option. On the surface it looked like there was no way that we could get this merger done in ninety-seven days. Impossible…or so it seemed. It reminded me of a phrase in an Ella Fitzgerald song that my husband told me about once: "The difficult we will do right away, the impossible might take a little longer!"

So as I ate, I finalized my strategy in my mind. "Guys, do you trust me?"

My colleagues, Lee and Ray, were all ears now and could see that I was committed.

I spoke my thoughts out loud: "We need to put all the things that need to get done on one list for everyone to see. We need to put all the teams in a structure so that they can work together. We need to get everyone working on the ninety-seven-day plan at 150 miles an hour by tomorrow. We need to create an environment where success is the only option, and we need to do it all with a happy team that will work twenty hours a day for the next ninety-seven days to get it all done."

Lee and Ray agreed, but thought I was playing "master of the obvious."

I finished that delicious dinner and said, "What about this: We know that we do not have time to do traditional project plans and organization charts to align everyone on the team, but we have to get them all aligned to the same work and goals. So what if we take the principles of the process and make them live for real? We can make it life-size for all of the team to see, instead of waiting for the hundreds of pages explaining every line.

"We list everything that the teams need to be assigned, aligned by their roles and structure, all on one gigantic piece of paper. It's a visual aid for everyone so that we can teach them the process, the roles, and the work, all at the same time, so that by the time it's on one piece of paper we can have everyone aligned to the vision. And we will put this gigantic 'what to do' diagram all on the wall at the back of our work room." I could picture it all in my mind, but was not sure if I was adequately explaining my vision. "Well, what do you think?" I asked.

The guys thought I was a bit out there, but they knew we had to find a creative, yet appropriate, way to get this done. I could see it all in my head and had to make my idea clear to them.

We kept eating and I kept explaining.

"One enormous piece of paper for the whole project for all to see: a WALL, forty feet long by twelve feet high."

The guys went along with the idea. They could see that I was committed, that I had connected, and that I cared. I did care. In fact, I was excited. I was fully committed now, too. I felt the fire in my belly…now I needed to get everyone's belly fired up as well. What a day that next day would be. The village was about to be built, pulled together to make this miracle happen. I knew that we could do it.

Lee, Ray and I were about to form a type of "three musketeers" leadership to get this done. We each had our role. We each knew the challenge and we were willing to do anything to help the teams from both firms succeed in the merger. We needed to get to the teams from both companies quickly and communicate our vision, as unorthodox as it might be.

Now I just needed to break the news to my hubby…I was about to be staying in London for the long haul.

Chapter 3

STEP TWO: Form the Winning Team

So here you are! You have signed up for the challenge. You have embraced the challenge and have committed to the journey ahead of you, but still have an incredible amount of work to do. You still need to Form the Winning Team, Be the Leader, Stock up on Your Soft Skills and Make It Happen.

Regardless of the challenge, the team is the key. There are projects that you sign up for where you can build your own team, and there are teams that you inherit and need to make your own. Not to worry. This chapter is all about forming that winning team regardless of how long you've been working with them. YOU CAN BUILD AND MOBILIZE A "GET IT DONE" KIND OF TEAM!

1. **Embrace the Challenge**
2. **Form the Winning Team**
3. **Be the Leader**
4. **Stock up on the Soft Skills**
5. **Make It Happen**

A CLICHÉ OR A REAL STEP?

Most of my work in recent years has been focused on leading teams in crisis, and usually the teams and the project are faced with an almost insurmountable challenge or several challenges. This crisis experience provides me with constant validation of why "forming a winning team creates success" is not a cliché. It is cold, hard fact.

Forming a winning team sounds on the surface like we are building an organizational structure, but the reality is that it is so much more. Remember that in this book, we are focusing on the how and not the what, which means that all that you already know about building an organization should only be enhanced by these additional thoughts. It's about mobilizing the team in a balanced way, with all aspects of the team in mind.

All teams should be built to achieve *any* goal and to handle *any* problem or challenge. Projects can be very easy and face very few challenges, or they can be constantly struggling and face every problem that can be expected and, of course, some that aren't. How you approach forming your team will pay off in spades with each passing issue or challenge.

In order to make the argument that this step is critical to

successful delivery, let's take a look at one of my favorite movies, *Apollo 13*. It also happens to be a true story.

You can build a team and follow all your technical training, but if your team is not set up in such a way as to handle disasters and crises, then they will only be mediocre in daily delivery. The Apollo 13 example illustrates to me that the best and most well-rounded teams will ride through any challenge they face. Because it is such a great illustration of all that I believe in, *Apollo 13* is a must-see for all of my teams.

The Apollo 13 mission was a several-year project and the final "go live" moment was when everything would be proven. This is the same for most projects in the world, even those outside of NASA. Months and months, even years, are spent working towards the goal of a launch day, whatever the launch may be. Most of us are not launching rockets, but there is the day when the "GO" is given. It's all in the delivery, but that delivery is the result of much time and effort.

The example I would like to bring to your attention is at the point in the story when the space mission had been given its go and everyone cheered. The initial moment of launch happened as planned and all indications were that it appeared to be a success. It's in the middle of the mission that there were issues that generated concern. That was the point when they discovered a catastrophic scenario facing them. The moment of truth came from one leader to another. The leader in space said what is now a famous sentence to the leader on the ground: "Houston, we have a problem."

Well, it turns out that the Apollo 13 mission had more than a problem; they had many. Master alarms were going off everywhere. And then came the staggering diagnosis: The astronauts could all die. The objective of the Apollo 13 mission was no longer to land on the moon; it was to save the lives of the crew.

Many of us work on critical projects and some of us may even be involved in projects that are life and death situations. No matter what the level of grim importance may be in our own projects, the rationale and philosophy remain the same.

No matter what, the leader needs to be cool and collected to keep the team on that same calm wavelength. All technical methodologies and project management processes have flaws, and with Apollo 13, the process for readying the team for safe return was also flawed. This is where the critical element of TEAM allows for survival and success. The ability of the team to pull together is what saved the lives of those astronauts, not the technical processes and methodologies and checklists that NASA had spent millions on. Those factors are fundamental and significant, of course, but the most vital component was ultimately the team.

The leader in charge on the ground, the head of mission control, said something very key: "Let's stay cool, people. I want everyone to alert your support teams. Wake up anybody you need to and get them in here. Let's work the problem. Let's not make things worse by guessing."

He kept everyone focused and cool, and he knew that the teams he'd formed had the capacity and capability to solve the problem. His job was to lead them through the crisis in a calm and direct way. I can only imagine what he must have been thinking, and I'm pretty sure that at that moment of crisis he felt some relief from the quality and competence of the high-performing team that he had built.

A well-designed team understands that "failure is not an

option." A good leader leads the team to that goal. When in a crisis, the experience and capability of the team members will surely provide a million different ideas for how to get out of the current trouble facing the project. This is when crucial decision-making ability comes into play. This is also the point when some people succeed and some people fail.

The ability to make a decision at the turning point is easier said than done. If the proverbial shit hits the fan on "go live" day, you as the leader have to dig deep into your gut and, along with the advice of your team, you need to clearly think through all the options to determine the right thing to do. "Thinking on your feet" is a skill that all leaders need to develop.

A well-formed team is able to address challenges and think out of the norm, and they can get through the tough times. And when the dust settles and you have emerged successfully on the other side, everyone can still shake hands and look each other in the eye.

Every project is like an obstacle course to maneuver. The best way to navigate is to be able to cut through the emotion and deal with the facts. You can bet there was a lot of emotion when those astronauts were trying to make their way back to planet Earth. The team on land trying to find solutions had to keep their emotions in check and deal with the facts, which was not easy, and when things got out of control, that's when the leader's knowledge of the team came into play.

He could calm them and focus them individually and as part of a team. He could even make a square peg fit into a round hole (that's my favorite part). For more on that, you will have to watch the movie. And if you have already seen *Apollo 13*, it's worth another viewing.

You may not be faced with forming the winning team for a space mission, but if you treat your team-building process like it is that important, then your team will be truly high-performing and will be unstoppable.

ADD TO YOUR LEADERSHIP TOOLKIT:

For this second step, forming a high-performing team, you will now add the tool that I call DEUCES to your toolkit.

"Deuces Never Loses"

I have developed a framework for forming the winning team that I call DEUCES. If you are a poker fan, you know that 'deuces never loses" is a phrase describing the odds of having deuces.

Well, in delivery, I can tell you the odds when using DEUCES to mobilize your team are even better!

1. **Embrace the Challenge Using the 3 Cs**
2. **Form the Winning Team With DEUCES**
3. **Be the Leader by Mastering the Art of Leadership**
4. **Stock up on the Soft Skills With the 4 Ls**
5. **Make It Happen With a Secret Formula**

DEUCES first helps you form the right mix for the team by focusing on the team's holistic makeup rather than simply their individual skills. In Project Knightsbridge, Lee, Ray and I were taking on a team already identified, but our job was to organize and mobilize the team in a way that they could succeed.

DEUCES helps you approach the forming of a winning team and build the culture you need to encourage performance excellence. This tool also then creates an awareness about the external influences that can corrode the team's foundation, and finally provides structure so all team members understand their role and their work.

Why do I call it DEUCES? It's an acronym for:

Disposition
Experience
Understanding
Culture
External Influences
Structure

DISPOSITION

DISPOSITION is how a person is wired. Here I go again, stating the obvious, but we all are wired differently. You want as many team members as possible to possess a positive "I can do anything" disposition. As a leader, you must recognize that trait in your team members.

Yes, technical skills are still important, but disposition should not be sacrificed for technical skills. A poor disposition can severely pollute a team and its productivity. A shaky disposition can be more detrimental to the project than shaky technical skills.

You must look at the disposition of each person on your team. You will notice that in the DEUCES way of forming the top team, the order of each attribute is on purpose and not by accident. What is number one in importance? Disposition! It is the absolute most critical component to a team succeeding in any challenge.

To evaluate disposition, there are several areas to understand and be aware of across your team. You need to: know the healthy disposition of a team member; know your natural leaders; know your change agents and, finally, know your rebels so you can turn them around.

Know the Healthy Disposition of a Team Member

Each team member is critical to the overall success of the team. I cannot stress that enough. You choose and mentor them by first understanding their innate abilities and honing their skills to the required role for the team. They first must exhibit certain qualities: commitment to the mission, loyalty to the team, and willingness to learn and improve.

Commitment to the Mission

An individual's commitment is something you should ask for and look for. Someone who is committed to the mission is always looking out for the most effective and creative ways to get things done, and will put their own personal goals out of mind and look at the right thing to do. For example, a person who holds a VP position on a team might be needed to do the work that would traditionally be done by someone who holds a lower-level title. The committed individual will not ever say any work is below them; they will do whatever is required to fulfill the mission. The person who says, "That's not my job" is not committed to the mission.

Loyalty to the Team

Loyalty is most evidenced when times of stress are in play. If the goals of the team are not being met, the loyal team player will avoid finger-pointing at all costs. They will look at ways to help their teammates achieve success instead of making themselves look better by blaming or scapegoating.

Willingness to Learn and Improve

We all can improve and we all have faults or weaknesses. Our willingness to join a team and meet the challenge is witnessed with our ability to openly address our weaknesses and not avoid them.

When individuals on the team and even the cultural leaders of the team know their own weaknesses, they will reach out for support from each other and allow others to fill in where needed. This allows the team to work through any challenge before it's too late.

When we have individuals with a disposition that displays an "I'm perfect" front, they will hide problems to protect themselves from others finding out their weaknesses. Trying to do that can potentially result in what could have been a tiny problem needing a simple resolution exploding into a much larger issue that can be detrimental to the team's success.

No one is perfect. Trying to pretend to be so is a waste of energy. Use that energy to learn and improve.

When you hear people say "attitude is everything," that is no joke. Attitude and disposition can make or break a team. For example, Sadie might have the right degree and the right work experience and the right references, but if her disposition is negative, you can't afford to have Sadie negatively impacting the other team members.

In Project Knightsbridge, the team was already on the ground, waiting for leadership and direction. The one thing they all shared with very few exceptions was their disposition. Lee, Ray and I were able to identify the cultural leaders and put them in positions of influence and this made the team stronger. The team as a whole was committed, loyal and willing to do anything to play their part in the project's success so we were very fortunate. We had a few instances when the disposition of one was negatively impacting others and we were able to identify it, address it and improve the situation.

We all like to be part of a winning team and that means that we don't want to see our efforts being compromised due to someone on the team who is putting our success at risk because they aren't willing to be a team player. That being said, if the negative Sadie is heartfelt, contrite, and committed to changing her approach, the team should be directed to support her and give her the opportunity to succeed with them.

Know Your Natural Leaders

You will be building a team that can essentially lead itself. You need to identify who will be your leaders for each aspect of the mission. The disposition of your team leaders will require a careful review.

Some people are natural-born leaders, like the example I gave earlier with Riley. Plain and simple, leading others is their gift. They have the ability to rouse people to action. They instigate healthy habits and create an encouraging atmosphere. How they relate to others almost seems effortless to them. It's easy to like being around this kind of person. Find these individuals, put them on your team and keep them.

Many times you might wonder how to quickly identify these individuals. The general signs are as follows:

1. Others look to them for support when they are in a crowd or meeting.
2. They will test you on your approach in public and in a healthy way.
3. They will not be afraid of a challenge and are usually the first to volunteer to help out on an issue.
4. They will not shy away from a conflict but try to solve the issue at the source of the problem.
5. They will be the natural "go to" people for any team members under stress.

Once you have identified your natural leaders and put them in a position of trust, leading on your behalf, it's critical that you mentor them in their leadership role to ensure that all the principles of disposition are managed throughout the team as a whole.

Know Your Change Agents

Natural change agents are absolutely brilliant additions to any high-performing team. These types of individuals have a disposition that is welcoming and comforting. They also have an innate ability to see where the old thinking needs to be pushed and where the panic may ensue with change, and, most importantly, they will be able to help the team embrace change in an open and safe way to ensure that no corners are cut because of fear.

In some cases with certain types of projects, it is unrealistic to specifically recruit change experts. When you don't have the dedicated role, and even if you do, building and championing change agents from within the team is incredibly valuable. For example, if you are restructuring a corporation's entire shipping department, including all processes, roles and responsibilities, then you definitely need to recruit the individuals with the specific experience for this type of work. But if you are managing a small project that is short in time with no specific mandate for change, then you would not recruit someone specifically for this role, so you must find them within your team.

In product development, for instance, you may have had ten years of the same look and feel for your marketing brochures. The thought may be "Why change what is not broken?" But if you have change agents identified as part of the disposition of your team, they might see that changing the brochure slightly might attract a new type of customer and increase your revenue.

There are many different types of change with any project or initiative. For instance, you can have process change and you can have it result in people change. The experts who identify and manage process change will be different than the experts you need to handhold people change. Know the difference and do not shortcut this need.

Team members who focus on change are a different breed; they think differently and they react to stress differently. As an example, someone who is a natural change agent and has a warm and motivating disposition can introduce change ideas to the team without creating competition and fear. This allows the team to engage and respond in an open way to the new ways of thinking, which will make encountering and maneuvering change easier for you and your entire team.

Know Your Rebels

Team members with a poor disposition exhibit no enthusiasm and lack a broader point of view. All indications seem to say that they don't enjoy their job. They have learned the textbook way of delivering, and they feel that that is "the" way, the only way.

When these team members are in a team environment, they can become domineering and demanding. If they are in a leadership role, the workplace may begin to feel like a dictatorship to employees. These leaders might hide in their office behind a closed door with a definite "No Entry" aura about the place. No one should want to be like that and no one should have to work with someone like that.

You then have two choices: retain or remove.

I believe that everyone should get a chance for change so you should always first reach out to this individual. Ask them if they want to be a member of this team and be a part of a successful mission. If they hesitate in responding or if you feel that he or she just can't make the leap and there is no time to help them improve their attitude without affecting the positive energy of the team, then you must make the hard decision to remove them from the team.

This is by far one of the hardest decisions you will need to make as the leader of a high-performing team, but it is critical that you do not waffle. The rest of the team must always know that everyone is accountable for the disposition they bring to the table each and every day.

I want to add that if you are in a position where an individual must be removed from the team, this is a very important growth moment and you should take the opportunity to provide leadership via open communication. This individual should understand why they are not a fit for the team at this time and how they can improve to become a fit in the future or a fit in other teams of which they may aspire to be a part.

In some cases, for instance, this individual may have been the star player, the lynchpin technically, and in the past rewarded for this contribution alone. He or she may have never been held accountable for their disposition or approach in being part of a team so this will be a new experience for them. Make your decision clear to the individual. It won't make them like you, but some day they may reflect and thank you for the openness and honesty. They could still end up on a future team of yours some day down the road.

EXPERIENCE

Experience is the knowledge of a topic, or skill in something gained through involvement in whatever that "it" may be. The history of the word "experience" aligns closely with the concept of experiment. So what does that mean? We learn by doing.

Experience is important and is the second cog in DEUCES.

The balance of depth of experience across your team is what is essential. We all have to start somewhere, without any real experience. We learn on the job and our ability to learn and our desire to learn outweigh how much actual experience a person has. The times and technology and crises are always changing. We are often faced with problems that have never been encountered before. Experience in handling crisis is equally important as actual technical experience.

Each generation looks at experience differently, and each generation is critical to the dynamics of the team. Effective leaders understand this sticky wicket of experience, and they hire people based not solely on technical expertise, but a three-fold criteria that includes skills, knowledge and history.

Skills

Skills are one piece of the experience pie. Skills should be looked at as the foundation for an individual's experience.

There are three angles for skills assessment on your team:

1. ***The balance of skills on your team:***
   The important thing to take into account regarding skills balancing is that everyone has a role to fill and each role is equally important. As a leader, it is your job to understand how best to balance your skills across your team.

   For instance, if we are building a bridge, we would need team members with skills in architecture, design and construction to start and these would be highly technical skills. The project for getting the bridge built would also need team members with delivery skills. These are the individuals on the team that know how to manage the work effort of all the detailed project plans, status reports and budgets.

   In addition to the technical skills experience and delivery skills experience, the team would also require members who hold it all together. In essence, these folks are the GLUE of the team.

   Another aspect, for example, when building a bridge would be the need for community liaisons that interface with the community on detour management or noise complaints during construction. These skills are not on the surface critical to the success of the project, but in fact they are what holds everything together for the whole team.

2. ***The résumés of the individuals on your team:***
   Many times you will be inheriting a team and not have had the chance to recruit and interview the team members yourself. For these cases, it is critical for you to work with your HR managers. Ensure that you have reviewed the résumés of the individuals on your team where the roles are specific enough to require that due diligence.

   Going back to the example of building a bridge, you may want to validate that the architects on the project actually have a résumé that backs up that role. Where the roles are less directly impacting the safety of the product being produced, use conversation and interaction to evaluate their résumés. The more critical aspect of the résumé is not the writing, but the next piece, which is the quality of the skill set.

3. ***The quality of the skills on your team:***
   This is the key area for skills validation, and as a leader, you should really be focused on the skill set. Your job is to understand which individuals on your team can assess skill set quality. In some cases, you would hold the experience to be able to query the level of quality, but in many cases, you would not.

   The important aspect of quality assessment is to ensure that you do not just assume that because the résumé looks good, the individual is suitably placed in the role. You need to verify and confirm the quality of their skills experience. Use others to help you in this confirmation process if needed.

Knowledge

Knowledge is different than skills.

Knowledge differs from skills because it suggests to me that the individual has taken a skill, like programming, and actually programmed a space shuttle launch pattern, for example. Knowledge is experience through applied skills.

In a computer development project, the skill sets that would be on the team would consist of individuals who had programming skills, but they may not have knowledge of how to program the particular end product that is being developed. The knowledge experience may or may not be critical, but must be assessed.

Some of the programmers would absolutely need to have experience and knowledge around the specific product or your project would be considered very quickly to be research-based and would possess more risk. On Project Knightsbridge, we needed to explicitly assess who had specific technical skills for programming our computers to technically handle merging the two companies' systems.

Each programmer did not have the same level of knowledge-based experience, but there were several senior programmers who did that were asked to mentor the others.

Another very important aspect of knowledge experience on Project Knightsbridge was the assessment of which team members held knowledge experience on mergers in the banking industry.

With the dynamics that were at play in a merger of this nature, we needed to reach out to external experts to enhance the team's experience. This ensured that when facing challenges, we also didn't have to face a steep learning curve.

As the leader, you must also make certain that knowledge can be positively applied in your team. Forming the winning team with individuals who have knowledge of the work must also go hand in hand with the first aspect of DEUCES, disposition. All team members need the right disposition as well. Samuel Johnson is quoted as saying, "Integrity without knowledge is weak and useless, and knowledge without integrity is dangerous and dreadful."

As a leader, you need to acquire the knowledge to be respected on the job, and then you need to live your life with integrity to best impart your knowledge to those around you. You want team members who follow this same philosophy as well.

History

You also need to consider history. When I am building my team, I look for the individuals on the team who either have a history with the clients we are working with, or perhaps history with the team that works for the company we are buying. We need history to apply our skills and experience in an appropriate way. For instance, when building the bridge, our community liaison would be even more successful if they had had a positive history working with the community.

As leaders, we must also be very open about our own inability to do everything well. That means we need to know our own skill gaps, knowledge gaps, and history needs, and then we will be able to put people around us who fill those gaps and give the team a greater chance for success.

It's a blending of all team players in the right proportion that creates a winning team. When all the team members can work together, have a good disposition, and rely on each other with a positive attitude, then they can each take their own skill set, knowledge, and history to the next level and truly form the greatest team.

<u>U</u>NDERSTANDING

A Top Team Must Understand Its Mission

I dug out my dictionary: Understanding (also called intellection) is a psychological process related to an abstract or physical object, a person, situation, or message whereby one is able to think about it and use concepts to deal adequately with that object.

Interesting. We want our team to be able to think and use concepts to deal adequately with the abstract and the physical. For me, these elements all tie together. We need the people on the team to understand the mission we are to accomplish and we need everyone to understand the abstract, the nuances of working with a team. Each person needs to be able to go off and do their work, and they need to be able to mesh with the team in the overall big picture.

Team members and leaders need a great disposition, balanced experience, and the understanding of the overall game plan. The team will be stronger if some key members also understand and have experienced what it is like to work under pressure so that when times get tough, several team members can support you in calming and directing the team as a whole.

Once you are sure that your team players are capable of

understanding then YOU, as the leader, must clearly relay the mission in a way that is absorbable and easy to internalize. You then identify your team leads or communication and change agents. They are the ones that truly can translate your mission, internalize it, and then generate further understanding across all team members and even outside influencers, such as clients. Generating understanding is a constant work effort. It needs to be managed every day throughout the entire process of delivery.

Understanding the political landscape that you are in and the way in which the team needs to maneuver is also an important aspect of selecting some key team leads. There must be members of your team that have the knowledge of the landscape and the understanding of the mission, and then they can be the glue that keeps your team together. When you build your team with clear thought on their roles with respect to understanding the mission and its political landscape, then the next piece of DEUCES will be easier because you know who is at the core of understanding the overall picture.

CULTURE

Your team needs a culture that is "fit to purpose." It's up to you, the leader, to create and cultivate it. Each member is coming from different backgrounds and has different views on how to get things done. Your job is to know them and know the mission, and then match them so that they are unstoppable. The team members must believe that they can achieve everything they need to in order to complete the mission successfully.

It's like a hockey game. A hockey coach works hard to build a culture among the team regardless of where the players had been before. They must make their mark and they must know their identity.

How do you build a culture with a team that is either new or newly formed?

- Communicate the Culture You Want
- Cultivate Pride
- Honor Ethics
- See the Results of a Healthy Culture

Communicate the Culture You Want

As the leader of the team, it is absolutely within your capability to direct a team of individuals to use their talents for good. If you have built the best team and do not manage the culture, arrogance will be obvious even if it is unintentional. The trick is to have pride without arrogance and competition without cutthroat tactics. Manners are also a key component of a great culture. So how do you cultivate and communicate to generate a healthy culture? Here are some ideas that work every time!

1. Lay a foundation of respect for all from day one: Culture has no hierarchy. Respect is required up, down, and sideways.
2. Meeting manners must be in place: People can be rude. You as the leader need to foster an approach

that does not allow rudeness. For instance, when I go into a meeting, I do not bring my cell phone. That meeting time is for those people in that room and we all need to dedicate ourselves to it. This is a show of respect for everyone and for their time.

3. Enforce rules through fun: Set meeting rules, charge charity fines and other 'fun' things so people know that time is valuable and respect for people's time is crucial. When I run a meeting, I don't want to be a police officer laying down the law. Instead, I put a process in place that I learned from Elliot on Project Knightsbridge and Elliot remains a friend today: "Okay, guys, we are going to raise money for charity. It's a good cause and here's how we do it. If someone's phone rings, that's five bucks. If someone talks while someone else is talking, that's five bucks. If you ask a question because you weren't paying attention and that question was answered an hour ago, that's ten bucks. If you fall asleep, that's twenty bucks." The chuckles begin, especially at the charge for falling asleep but believe me, in an all-day work session, we've raised some pretty nice coin for charity!

4. Hold each other accountable: As discussed above, instituting a charity fundraiser serves a dual purpose. You raise money for a good cause and the rules force the team to monitor each other's behavior with a sense of camaraderie. The other day when Jake fell asleep in the meeting and had to cough up twenty bucks, the whole group had a great laugh. Word gets

around. In the next meeting with a different group, they all had heard that someone had to pay the big fine and joked about who would fall asleep today. People hold each other accountable in a comfortable setting. It would be much more difficult for a team member to call someone out on bad behavior if it wasn't fostered openly. The team even holds me accountable. The other day, a colleague was talking and I was typing on my laptop. A coworker pointed out that my offense equaled talking when another was talking. She was right. I paid up. It's a good-natured way of keeping meetings on track and maintaining an atmosphere of respect.

5. Create pride in the work: Establish early deliverables that create a reason to 'show off the team talents' and create a cause for celebration. These little things early on are actually your teaching tools about what is expected and what is acceptable. That's a culture of pride in the team, pride in the work

6. Exhibit humility early: As the leader, be the first to say, "I don't know the answer to this." Don't hesitate to tell your team, "You guys are amazing." That's a culture of humility.

7. Introduce early and frequent decision points: It is highly effective and efficient to put in early and frequent decision points so that people always know the current information and are able to make decisions to influence direction. Create a 'decision-making' culture in which everyone participates. This is a

productive thing that you can do because it means you never get too far off track (or wasteful) and as a by-product, it reduces the opportunity for blame and negative behaviors.

Cultivate Pride

Pride is not vanity. Pride is good. We want to take pride in our work and we want to be proud of the company for which we work, as well as the team with which we work.

I have a friend who used to work for a government agency in the U.S. There were many good aspects to working for this agency, but there was no pride. The pay was great; the benefits were great; the work hours were great. The workload itself was not that bad, but Kim was surrounded by people who took no pride in their jobs.

The agency itself lacked pride. Morale was low. There was no team spirit. The managers were counting down the years until retirement. If you did a great job or an awful job, it didn't matter. Kim tried to convince herself that it was an easy job with good money, but she longed to have pride in her work and the place she worked. The discouraging feeling outweighed all the perks, and Kim left the agency to find employment elsewhere.

Pride is essential. All people want it and the upcoming generation demands it! The newcomers into the workforce have high expectations and rightfully so. This is the pool from where the next world leaders will emerge. We want them to be tech savvy and still remain in touch with their own humanity. This new generation is defiantly optimistic and positive about the future and the way they feel that it "ought" to be. I, for one, am encouraged by what I see in today's young people.

Take Pride in the People on Your Team

A good leader will recognize leadership potential in another and will want to help bring that out. A good leader wants to give rise to more good leaders. A good leader takes pride in the people on their team and mentors individuals to become future leaders.

Mentoring is a good thing and the best kind of mentor relationship is where a colleague sees what an individual is doing for the team, the pride they take in their work, and then aids them in building their future goals. You should know that as a leader, this individual that you reach out to mentor feels honored that you have taken an interest in their career. You, as the mentor, will also feel good about teaching and creating another generation of leaders. This way of starting a mentor relationship is a recipe for success.

If you are in a position of leadership now, start looking around for leadership potential in others. Simply paying attention goes a long way. When you tune in, you see. And when others see that you recognize something in them, they spark. They thrive. They grow. When you identify talent, it's amazing how it really begins to shine. The best leaders grow more leaders.

Honor Ethics

My mission with this book is not just about the workplace and people as team members; my scope is larger. We need to use these people skills in all interactions, with all people. We need to be ethical in all of our dealings, with everyone, in every situation. It keeps things simple for one thing, and it simply is the right thing to do.

"There's harmony and inner peace to be found in following a moral compass that points in the same direction regardless of fashion or trend." Ted Koppel said that. He is so right. Following that moral compass will lead you out of many tangled webs.

Maybe some business executives need to see that being ethical is actually good for the bottom line. In a sense, it is actually self-serving to be ethical. I like to think that companies are ethical because it is the right thing to do. I also know that companies are run by people, and I think that people should be ethical because it is the right thing to do.

"Proactive ethics" is a term I use to mean an active empathy, actually searching for opportunities to do better for your staff and community—not only responding to staff feedback taken in annual polls, but thinking and feeling on your own with the mindset to discover what the needs might be. So much of life boils down to mindset.

Management needs to understand that they can have this very same effect on their staff. Morale is an incredibly powerful source of untapped, renewable energy. As company morale goes, so does company productivity. If management were to lead in a proactively ethical style, they would see a collective boom in productivity, quality, ideas and community reputation.

People deliver results most efficiently and solidly in an open, creative,transparent, and honest environment. It is only common sense that companies that have a poor reputation will have difficulty attracting and retaining the best workers.

Everyone, no matter what their background may be, operates under a code of personal principles. Call it morals, call it ethics, and call it the difference between right and wrong. We know what the right thing to do is, even if it is difficult.

If you work for someone you don't respect, someone you don't trust, you may find that the ethical culture at all levels mimics that of the top rung. The attitude can become "if the boss is a crook, why should I care?" If the top dogs don't care, it trickles down. It's hard to keep caring if you feel like your efforts don't matter. As a leader, you have to constantly monitor your own actions and attitudes. The team is often a mirror image of what they see happening in leadership. Use this for good.

Give them what they want. People want ethics. Be a person of integrity. You will get people of integrity who will want to work with you. Like attracts like.

See the Results of a Healthy Culture

Commitment Will Shine

Commitment can be seen from miles away. When a group of individuals works for the same team, but each one is only out for their own goals, it's clear that their commitment is not to the project, but to their own future. When that culture is allowed, and sometimes even developed, then all will appear to be well until the "impossible" needs to be accomplished.

Interestingly enough, individuals who are committed to the team will shine as well and succeed in their career organically.

Again, it goes back to trust. Let' say hypothetically that Lee didn't trust me and I didn't trust him because we knew that each of us was only out for our own careers. If we never needed to rely on each other, all would be okay. But let's say that we are trying to solve a major problem that has to be fixed in a matter of hours. If we don't solve it, the project as a whole, and the team as a whole, is at risk. Where, then, would that get us? All of a sudden, it's critical that Lee and I work together. Now we need to have a commitment that is beyond our own personal career goals.

I used Lee and myself as examples, but in fact we trust each other implicitly. We were teased all the time on Project Knights-bridge because we were so aligned that people looked at us as brother and sister. We even shared a desk together in the middle of the floor where everyone on the team worked so that we would be seen as a true partnership in delivery leadership. Trust isn't something that you can pretend to have. It must be real and it must be evidenced by actions.

If Lee and I hadn't started being able to trust and rely on each other from the beginning, we would have not been able to work effectively with each other when crunch time hit. There were several times that Lee was the one who was able to help me see the way through a difficult time. At one very difficult time in the project, Lee and another colleague Ryan will remember dragging me out to the Hard Rock Café for a bite to eat to help me strategize a complicated and political situation. You need to rely on your colleagues to act as your sounding board and trust that your weaknesses will be made stronger for it.

Commitment by each individual to each other and the mission means that no one can penetrate the team in a negative way. The team can then sustain through stressful times. Think of commitment as the project's vitamin C. It is like a vitamin to avoid a cold; commitment prevents neglect and resentment.

Maneuvering Obstacles Will Be Easier

In leadership, it can be one person begging everyone to get through difficult times. The leader of the team must be the guide through these rough patches, but the group of individuals all need to know how to rely on each other and work without the one leader.

Do we have team members who only like to work with the boss? Or do we have team members that like to partner with each other under the guidance of the boss? Guidance is good, but handholding through every situation is not necessarily a good thing. The team needs leadership and needs to be able to function independently.

In the beginning of any new team-building phase, the leader needs to be the one micro-maneuvering, but after a bit of on-the-job experience and tutoring by the leader, the team should form a maneuvering masterpiece on its own.

The Upcoming Generation Will Be Attracted

It is my goal for all of us to agree that you can do anything if you understand people.

Read that sentence again. Let it sink in. You can do anything if you understand people.

That statement is as true today as it was a hundred years ago. Even in our modern wired world, we need to understand people. The psychology of this next up and coming generation is that of innovation, instinct, and integrity.

The next generation wants new ideas and better ways of accomplishing tasks, they want to follow their instincts and trust that they can solve problems, and they want to maintain their dignity and respect. That is not asking for too much and it is exactly what we should give them. Yes, they are more wired than any previous group of people, but man cannot exist on technology alone. Technology is wonderful, but people make it happen.

The world of technology is working in a way that actually makes it harder for people to connect. That may sound contradictory to the general notion that "the world is getting smaller." Yes, we can talk to Tokyo without leaving the conference room, but the constant use of email, handheld devices, text messaging, etc. makes it harder for humans to connect on a human level.

One-to-one conversation is still important. Face-to-face meetings are still important. People are still people, with a heart and soul, and we can't ignore that. With all the modern marvels that the next generation takes for granted, they still long for a personal connection.

EXTERNAL INFLUENCES

Be very "360 degrees" in building your team. Look at all the angles. Every leader must institute a parallel of equals. People are not one-dimensional and your teams will reflect this. People are also influenced by people and attitudes around them.

Social influence is an easy example. In a nutshell, social influence is when the actions or thoughts of individuals are changed by other individuals. Examples of social influence can be seen in socialization and peer pressure. This is the effect of other people on a person's behavior. Social influence is also a type of persuasion. A person may behave a certain way because he follows the persuasive demeanor of another.

As a leader, you have to be cognizant of all the external influences affecting your team. External influences can derail a team from focus almost immediately. A client screaming, a local resident yelling in a town hall meeting, or a bad set of publicity hitting the initiative you are working with are all outside forces that can bring down the team morale and momentum.

As important as defining your team members who will work full-time on the project, the external influences affecting your team need to be defined and understood. Once the external influences are identified, all team members must then be openly supported in order to understand their external influences. This requires full transparency on the part of the leader and all cultural leaders on the team. The team members need to feel free to come to you with any issues that may impact the team via external influences and you can then help them manage the situation.

There are several examples where external influences are good energy for the team, but there are also many situations where negative energy is exposed to the team. Many negative situations are a result of misunderstanding on the part of individuals who aren't intimately involved in the project and result in fear-based actions.

Fear-based actions don't get things done and can result in political situations that can be very detrimental for the productivity of the team. For example, if someone who is an external influence doesn't like the initiative you are working on, they may use water cooler talk to try to shut it down. If the culture is already established with your team and your team knows who has what role, they can openly discuss the rumors with the communication lead on the team and talk through the "scary stuff." Then an appropriate, real and non-gossipy approach can be taken to alleviate this individual's concern.

Sometimes the external influencing force is a person who tries to be disruptive in their attacks, but does not succeed. If the team is equipped to deal with the potential problem brewing, then you can create an energy in the team that truly illustrates to this external influencer that your team members are all on the same page and no division can come out of their efforts.

A great example would be how President Obama dealt with all the outside influences while running his campaign. He was the epitome of calm, cool, and collected. He kept a level head and a steady image. The media often stated that President Obama was able to avoid many problems because he and his team were never off script.

There really was no script per se. They were not reciting canned words or spewing lies. They were giving a consistent message all across America. President Obama, the leader, and his campaign manager had a vision, a clear culture, and tens of thousands of people representing the Obama bid for the presidency.

DEUCES was exemplified perfectly. The disposition of President Obama, and his staffers, was tremendously positive. Their experience was in the right places and they had an understanding of the political landscape and all of its nuances. The culture of their crew was in place early in the campaign and the external forces were also understood. The structure of President Obama's team was amazing. Much has been hyped about the grass roots efforts and the use of technology (emails and texting supporters), but the structure was indeed impressive. The organization and efficiency of communication all led to a successful campaign.

As a delivery expert, I watched and was pleased that the concepts and principles that I adhere to worked on this grand scale. My admiration for this team is strong. It also encourages me that these tools work. No matter how large or small your team or your mission, these delivery methods can work for you, too.

On Project Knightsbridge, we didn't face media scrutiny, but we did have the situation of two organizations merging. When mergers happen, there are some individuals who are worried about what the newly integrated company will look like and how it will impact their jobs in the long run.

The leadership team and I worked very hard to understand where these worries may source from and how they might impact the project team. With less than a hundred days to complete the project, it would have been severely damaging if negative energy impacted the team directly.

The first thing we did was identify all the key change agents and the key cultural leaders that would handle communication and strategy for the merger. Understanding and managing the outside influences of the team can be tricky, but it will pay off in the long run and will help the team maintain momentum while managing the outside influencers' expectations and keeping the team comfortable as well.

STRUCTURE

Structure is defined as a fundamental and sometimes intangible notion covering the recognition, observation, nature, and stability of patterns and relationships of entities. From a child's verbal description of a snowflake, to the detailed scientific analysis of the properties of magnetic fields, the concept of structure is an essential foundation of nearly every mode of inquiry and discovery in science, philosophy, and art.

I love that definition. I love structure. As much as I appreciate the freedom of brainstorming and as much as I realize how many things are out of our control, I still love structure. We need to have some kind of structure in place and freedom to move within that structure.

A structure defines what a system is made of. It is a configuration of items. It is a collection of interrelated components or services. The structure may be a hierarchy (a cascade of one-to-many relationships) or a network featuring many-to-many relationships. No matter what, all the pieces of the puzzle and all the players on the team need some kind of structure.

Structure lends itself to the team and the project being self-sustaining.

1. All people need to know they are contributing to the success of others and themselves.
2. Everyone needs to trust that they are operating in an open and transparent environment.
3. People must know what is going on at all times and not feel left in the dark.
4. Every individual needs to know their role, their purpose, and how to succeed.

All people operating in a group environment need to know the boundaries that they are expected to work within and what the social rules are, without getting stung by them unexpectedly. A good structure provides this safety net.

Structure as a Foundation

The combinations of dynamics on a team are limitless. A good structure can help manage these dynamics. Some people need more structure than others do, but we all need a framework of reference from which to operate. Individuals need to be able to "get their bearings" and providing structure can do that. We have instincts for a reason. We should use them. The more we do, the better honed they get.

As an effective leader, you will be interacting with everyone on the team. You will get to know them and know their strengths and weaknesses. The more equipped you are, the better equipped they are. It is better to be equipped before having to go into crisis mode.

Floundering in a job position with no clear idea of what to do is a motivation killer. If you can make it clear to team members who is responsible for what and by when, everyone becomes instantly happier and more productive. Clear expectations, no matter how large, are easier to handle than not knowing what in the heck is expected. This lack of structure can plague any size organization. Even teams with a small amount of members need clear definition of tasks.

In Project Knightsbridge, we had ninety-seven days until our "go live" day, the deadline for the merger to be complete. As I reviewed in Chapter 1, we had to take an extreme approach that was creative and much different than what the teams were used to. We referred to the "big" idea as The Wall. The Wall took into account the structure of the team and the work the team had to deliver, but it was still at the root based on valid organizational principles.

Whatever approach you use for documenting and communicating your structure for your team, make sure you do it so that everyone knows their role, and also knows each other's roles. People work more effectively in any given structure if they know how their role interrelates with the other roles on the team.

Decision Strategy Is the Glue in Any Structure

Time and time again, I have been called in to a project where there has been no real direction, no guidance. That is demoralizing for all involved. You can have the most perfectly analyzed and implemented organizational structure, but if you do not have a decision strategy or a clear understanding of how decisions are made, the team begins to spin.

The spinning of the wheels while waiting for a decision to be made is a waste of time and drains the energy of the entire team. In some cases, it's really bizarre when a decision has in fact been made, but not communicated; it's almost like management thinks the troops will hear it through the grapevine. Even more bizarre is that they think that is an acceptable way to lead and communicate.

The skill of a good leader is the ability to make a decision and communicate it. That takes confidence. If you waver a bit in your self-confidence right now, it will improve with time. There is a saying that courage is like a muscle; it gets stronger with use. Decision-making is the same. When you take the helm and make a decision, you will see that the sky didn't fall down, and you will feel more confident with each decision you make. You will also see that the team is actually relieved that a decision has been made and everyone can finally move forward.

When making a decision, you have to wipe out all ulterior motives. The only determining factor is what is best for all, what is best for the project. If ever there was a nugget of wisdom I want to pass on, it is this: Ask yourself this simple question before you have to make any decision—What is the right thing to do?

In order to do so, you must cut the emotion and deal with the facts.

That simple question is always the compass to guide by, in any area of life. It's what we teach our children and it's what we need to remember, no matter how complicated the issue is or how much money is involved or what is at stake. What is the right thing to do?

My strategies are not complex. But I think that maybe many projects are so messed up because people complicate things more than they need to. Simply focus on the essence of every issue and focus on your frame of mind. It's about trust; it's about caring; and it's about doing the right thing, no matter what.

BACK TO DELIVERY

Okay, back to London and Project Knightsbridge.

On Project Knightsbridge, we didn't have the time to take the team through fun exercises to bond them with each other and me with them; nor did we have much time to really focus on the individual aspects before sizing up the challenge. So we had to find a way to pull all of the team together and still get the project delivered by the deadline. We had to find a way to blend everything and produce results. It was an interesting challenge.

We were going to do this thing, the new idea we called The Wall. We pulled the teams together, but first we had to physically navigate the landscape and do some office rearranging. We moved all of the cabinets out of the way of the wall and then we rolled out brown paper and papered an entire wall.

I have to tell you the mere event of papering such an expanse of wall brought everyone together in an entertaining moment and they had no idea what was about to go on. Then with the paper on the wall, I drew the lines, up and down. The horizontal row was the teams with their work assignments, and the vertical columns were each week. Picture in your mind a huge grid. A huge, wall-size grid.

We used multi-colored sticky notes to identify the work by each team for each week. Then the teams huddled together to analyze their workloads and break them into one-day segments within each week.

Ninety-seven days…forty feet of paper…and goodness knows how many stickies.

There it was, eight hours later, The Wall. Every team knew their work, and what was due by when. That's a remarkable feat and it was accomplished in eight hours. How many teams take weeks to figure out what the heck they're doing? We simply didn't have the luxury of time.

It was encouraging to see The Wall take shape. It was also frightening to see what had to be done in our short timeline. The next thing on our to-do list was to make it happen and actually deliver the merger.

Today I still use The Wall approach. It's evolved to be THE WALL FOR LIVE THINKING WORK. For Project Knightsbridge, time was critical. I took all aspects of my technical training and tried to put a living, breathing side to the data that needed to be internalized by everyone on the team. By integrating the structure of the teams, the roles they play, the work that they needed to complete and the timeline we were stuck with, all of it on a life-size wall, each team member could understand their own work and also how their work was part of the overall mission.

It would have been nice to include a picture of The Wall for you to understand what I am trying to explain, but all photos of this masterpiece were later destroyed on 9/11 in New York City. That's a whole other story where amazing teams and leaders worked tirelessly to get miraculous things accomplished.

Now, in Project Knightsbridge, we also used The Wall to track the status of the work as well. One of our team members, Josh, laughed that he was so well paid for keeping status with sticky notes. Yep, sticky notes; no time for the proper technology tracking methodology. Today I use state-of-the-art tools and top-notch planning teams, but back then we had to reach out to creative options. (But between you and me, on every program or division mission that I lead, if I could find a wall big enough, I would still choose to use The Wall in its original display.)

The beauty of The Wall showing the live status was a morale boost. When a deliverable was completed, the green status sticker was replaced with a large check mark. Seeing those check marks was a lifeline some days to the team, and gave them hope that the goal could be reached. We had over 200 people all together on one floor wasting no time on status reporting and interpretation of status, but instead working on the incredibly challenging work and the very aggressive timeline.

Motivation from The Wall was what we used every day to keep people in sync with how things were going and when things looked behind. There were no secrets. Everyone could see a red status sticker from far across the room. When an area was in trouble, the whole team knew it and pitched in.

This brings up another point that I need to make. People also need to be held accountable for their work, their piece of the puzzle, without feeling scrutinized or that the finger of blame is ready to point to them.

To make the process easier, I also developed a quality checklist for each deliverable. This was a generic way for every team member to check, check, check that the component was complete before it could be deemed complete on The Wall. This method removes any blame or finger-pointing. Every person for every piece of the puzzle goes through the checklist. If something can't be checked off, they have to go back and get it done correctly. It's a reminder and it's quality control. It's the same for everyone. It supports the motto of all good projects: "It's all for one and one for all."

For Project Knightsbridge, one of the team members also put up a daily countdown on the wall starting at ninety-seven days. At the end of the day, we ripped off the page. Ninety-six days. End of the day, rip off the page. Ninety-five days. And so on. We always knew where we stood and what the time crunch was.

Maybe this all seems like common sense to you. In fact, I hope so. If so, you are ready to lead.

Chapter 4

STEP THREE:
Be the Leader

I have the habit of repetition. People matter. I've said it a lot. It's the golden thread of this book, and my very mission. If you've mastered the "people matter" foundation in your home life, keep that thought and apply it to how you lead.

1. **Embrace the Challenge**
2. **Form the Winning Team**
3. **Be the Leader**
4. **Stock up on the Soft Skills**
5. **Make It Happen**

The next step is to learn how to take your commitment to people to the next level in delivery. Leading a team of individuals is a daily challenge. Some people may think that everyone who takes a leadership role wakes up as a leader and goes to work every day and just does the job. It requires constant thought, focus, creativity and patience.

HOW SHOULD YOU BE LEADING?

Delivering results is a team effort and teams consist of people. (Yes, my children tell me that I have a knack for stating the obvious and for repetition, repetition, repetition.) The basic foundation of getting things done is learning how to treat people so you can motivate them to achieve the goals that have been set out for you and your team.

I want to shout it from the rooftops: Companies who hire leaders that embrace the fundamental concept that people matter will have a consistent competitive advantage. Adopting this style of leadership, and training new leaders who believe that people matter, can be *the* single defining factor in greater professional and personal success. It's not the latest gizmo or advance in technical know-how or speeding up the process that gives someone the edge. It's centuries-old people power.

I have now had the opportunity of seeing what my children also think about the workplace. Two of my three children have been in the workforce for a bit and both of them have had bad experiences with companies that do not embrace the concept that people matter.

Both of my children have given me the most amazing insight into what it is like to see the current leadership approaches from a young person's vantage point. They have said how demoralizing it has been to see that the management only cares about their job, the company only cares about profits, and the morale of the team is almost at the bottom of the priority list.

On the flip side, they have also given me examples of where they have felt supported and respected. They were willing to stay later and work harder because they felt like their manager cared about their contributions. I'm glad to see that this book might also give my children some insight into how they can make a difference as well.

Deciding to be a leader means being committed to understanding every aspect of leadership. Your main focus is not always about the task at hand; it is also about:

1. Being committed to the dynamics of the individuals as well as the team they are part of to meet a goal;
2. Always leading the individuals on your team to work together;
3. Wanting to know more about the people whom you are leading;
4. Never treating your team members like they are nameless, faceless worker drones;
5. Knowing that every individual is looking at you to help them learn about each other and form a team.

IT'S LIKE THE FIRST DAY AT SCHOOL

As I write this chapter, the timing is fascinating because I'm embarking on a new role in a project that I'm undertaking. What is perfect timing is the fact that this new role requires me to remember why I coined the word "peopledemia" in the first place. (We'll get into that in more depth coming up.) This new role is a golden opportunity to practice what I preach and to apply these concepts laid out here from scratch.

It's like starting the first day of school, really. There are dozens of new faces and new personalities to reconcile. In a leadership position, it's a bit more complicated because you have to get them to trust you and be open to you so you can help them succeed.

The Team Will Size You Up

When people are sizing up a new leader, they look for five things.

1. *They need to know that you are what you say you are:* There can be no mystery. Say what you mean and stick to it. Transparency is very important. People can sniff out ulterior motives in no time. If the team feels you are out for yourself, there will be no teamwork and there may be mutiny before you even get rolling.

2. *The team needs to understand you and your vision:* You have to prove that you will communicate. Then

they will communicate with you. Tell it like it is. No sugarcoating. No lying. No spinning. If you are open and honest every time, they will learn that they can be, too.

3. ***The team needs to know you will be calm in a crisis:*** In my case, I am usually coming in at the crisis point, so people are already on edge. I have to be the calm in the storm, not create more waves and not react emotionally to bad news or big issues.

4. ***You must be accountable for your actions:*** This one is a biggee. When you make a mistake, and you will, own up to it right away. If you admit your failings, you stop the negative chatter before it can start. There is a lot of groundwork to cover when starting with a new team. They don't know you. They will not automatically trust you.

5. ***You must make the hard decisions:*** For example, there can be an occasion when someone needs to be removed from the team for the good of all. This can be a hard situation, but as always, cut the emotion and deal with the facts. If the team member is not right for the project, it does not benefit the team, the project or the individual to keep them on. It is a disservice to all and you can't lose sight of that. However, usually the team member can be reassigned to a better and more fitting role. It usually turns out to be a win-win situation for the individual and for the team and the project delivery. There will be many

times when the leader needs to be ready to make hard decisions and the team needs to know you are up for the challenge.

ADD TO YOUR LEADERSHIP TOOLKIT: THE ART OF LEADERSHIP

The ability to lead people, the ability to make anything happen with a group of people with differing skills and personalities, is an exceedingly important skill for the twenty-first century. It can relate to a business, to the school, to your family dynamics, to anything. Sure, we have technology today that is practically science fiction, but even with all the gizmo gadgets we may think are irreplaceable, we still have to interact with people.

What is cutting-edge today may be obsolete tomorrow. One thing that will never be obsolete is our need to work together, despite our differences. "Plays well with others" is still on the kindergarten list of needed skills. We never outgrow the need to play well with others.

You can use the ART of Leadership as an additional tool set to enhance your skills and support this third step in the delivery methodology.

1. **Embrace the Challenge Using the 3 Cs**
2. **Form the Winning Team With DEUCES**
3. **Be the Leader by Mastering the Art of Leadership**

4. **Stock up on the Soft Skills with the 4 Ls**
5. **Make It Happen With a Secret Formula**

THE ART OF LEADERSHIP:
Appreciation
Respect
Trust

Appreciation

One of the most basic needs in human relationships is the need to feel appreciated. This need is present in every member of any company, committee, or family. Appreciation is the key to a feeling of self-worth and positive energy. It costs nothing to show and a little goes a long way.

A person who receives approval and feels that they add value will do more to contribute to the success of the cause—not because they feel pressure to do so, but because they will feel that their skills are an important part of a successful product or project delivery. People may perform under pressure, but they thrive with appreciation.

Most volunteer committee coordinators know this fact. Volunteers certainly don't do it (whatever "it" is) for the money, so if they don't feel appreciated, they will eventually move on to another organization that does express its appreciation. As the leader of the project team, you need to believe that it's important that everyone involved always feels like a worthwhile contributor, because when they do, they will remain enthusiastic and ready for the next task or project.

I've found that individuals on a team who feel appreciated will be much more productive, and that they will also tend to be an excellent influence on other team members as well as people in your organization outside the team. This effect will get you labeled as a leader who develops leaders, and that's a good thing. That is the very idea.

Appreciation is something that "rubs off." If you feel like you are appreciated, you are in a frame of mind that helps you see and appreciate what others around you are doing. You in turn will show your appreciation for their hard work and that will rub off on them. They then will pass on the appreciation, like the handoff of the Olympic torch, going from place to place, person to person, like a warm, vibrant light.

Respect

Appreciation and respect go hand in hand. As a good leader, you need to foster appreciation and respect as a two-way street. No one wants a boss that they don't respect, and respect cannot be demanded or commanded. You must earn it.

One of the best ways to earn respect is by respecting every team member, and acknowledging their contributions to an enterprise. One of the fastest ways to lose the respect of team members is by failing to take the time to acknowledge a contribution or, worse, to take credit for another person's contribution.

Employees who are respected and appreciated will respect and appreciate their co-workers, leaders, and company.

Think about how you go about your day. In your morning rush, do you tend to bark at your children or significant other in a tone you would never use with someone you don't know or are intimidated by? When you run in to pick up your dry cleaning, do you see a person behind the counter or do you just hand your ticket over without even giving a glance? Have you ever caught yourself talking on your cell phone and ignoring the living, breathing human being in your presence? You know the scene I'm talking about: "It's just the cashier."

One of the greatest life lessons that should permeate all aspects of our lives is that each of us should actively acknowledge that people matter, all people. The person that you are dealing with at any moment in time is just as important as the next, whether it's your boss, your peer, your secretary, your teenage son, or the clerk at the coffee shop. No matter the position— CEO, sanitation worker or stay-at-home mom—that person is doing their particular job to the best of their ability and that person wants, and needs, to be treated like a valued human being.

How can we show respect? Make eye contact. Listen. Be engaged.

That means not talking on the phone when you are with someone else. It means a smile and a friendly "thank you." It means manners, plain and simple. In these days of Blackberries and PDAs, this is getting even harder to stick to. Believe me, my children would say that I need to work on this, too.

Some managers have perused the requisite "handbook/quick guide" to leadership and give the "respect others" concept lip service at best. Or they say to themselves with a shrug, "Oh, yeah, of course I'm good to people. Let's move on." That doesn't work. People can sense sincerity, or the lack of it, from a mile away. Appreciation and respect are basic forms of caring.

Trust

There is a great quote that came from William Shakespeare: "Love all, trust a few, do wrong to none." I say you can trust more than a few, but "do wrong to none" are great words to live by. I would rather err on the side of trusting someone and have them let me down than to take the attitude of no trust. If you put your trust in someone, usually they will want to live up to it. Trust breeds trust.

If you operate under the assumption that you will do whatever it takes to get your job done and to get your people what they need, they will rely on you and trust you. When people trust you, you feel the strong sense to not let them down. You depend on each other and it's a win-win.

Trust is essential to any good relationship, working or otherwise, and makes it a relationship of reliance. A team relies on you as the leader to understand the team's goals and to empower the team to do the right thing, and they trust that you will stand by them when things don't go so well. Most importantly, the team needs to trust that they are not just a means to an end for you to climb the corporate ladder. The team needs to know that you will look out for them as a unit and individually. For you as a leader, this is a burden of trust that should not be taken lightly.

It also need not be a burden that is too much to bear. Every person, whether they hold a leadership role or not, will make mistakes. We're all human. Funny enough, it's the most effective leaders that are able to say, "Sorry, guys. I screwed up." The blame game is easy to play but will always cost you respect, because it's ineffectual and quite apparent to your team. Managers who generally find a scapegoat for problems and mistakes, instead of taking the responsibility themselves, wind up as one-project wonders because the best employees avoid working with them again if at all possible.

You are the leader. This is your team. You are one of them. You're all in it together. If your team is made up of full-time staff, part-time staff and consultant support, it doesn't matter. They are all your team—everyone is an equal part of the team. The cardinal rule I have in this area boils down to: Do not scapegoat; you take the heat. If something goes wrong, ultimately you are responsible. You are the team leader so it all comes back on your shoulders. So grow some pretty big shoulders right now.

Some mistakes are just stupid. Something falls through the cracks. Simple oversights that no one can believe went unnoticed. It happens. Those mistakes are humiliating but easy to fix. You as the leader must fess up. You go to your bosses and say, "I am sorry. It was stupid. We missed it. It's fixed. It won't happen again and we're moving on." Is it hard to go before the bosses and say that? Definitely, but there is no way around it. To stand up and point fingers at your team serves no purpose. It undermines the team and the execs don't care whose fault it is, they just want it fixed. If you stand up for your team, they will remember that. If you don't, you may never recover their trust.

If a project has a bottom line, it is not dollars—it is trust. It may sometimes seem simpler for you, the "boss," to be like a stage director of a play and say, "Now this is what you need to do. Go do it."

If you take this route, your team will not feel that you trust them and that you are willing to empower them to do the right thing. In the long run, better results are achieved if you as a leader can say, "What do you think you need to do? And what do you need to get it done?" Helping people to get their jobs done is the ultimate goal. Perhaps the better word for "boss" could be "helper." The leader is leading each individual to the desired end spot. The mentality is: This is where you need to be; how can I help you get there?

To put leadership principles into practice (the ART of leadership), the very notion of a leader gets turned on its head. The leader has to work for the team and not the other way around.

BACK TO DELIVERY

You want to be an effective leader and lead your team to prevail over all challenges and deliver the mission. You will also get it done while retaining peace and motivation among all levels of the team.

What happens when things don't go as smoothly as you had hoped and you and your team face overwhelming challenges? A general leadership approach is good in normal times but, boy, when times are tough and it seems impossible, you need that toolkit to be stocked.

The beginning of a moment of crisis or an "in trouble" project may sometimes seem formidable. If you are facing people who really don't understand each other and now have to work together, and you are the one to "make it happen," well, it can be daunting. I know this from experience. I gladly share my tales and tactics because I have come out on the other side. My experience is proof to me that what I say actually works.

At the end of it all, when the project wraps, there is a new respect for one another and a camaraderie that no one could have ever predicted in the beginning. There are so many people that I have been lucky to work with on extremely scary problems and we are still in contact today. Many of the people I worked with on Project Knightsbridge are still people I work with and also very good friends. It's amazing and so worth it. The work and patience required at the beginning of a new project with a new team is no doubt an uphill climb. But when you reach the peak, wow, what a great feeling.

Project Knightsbridge was a very difficult project because it was already in trouble, and it had an extremely aggressive timeline as well. The other complication with Project Knightsbridge was that it was a merger. In any merger, people integration in a hurry is difficult because realistically you don't have time to personalize your approach up front. I had always managed teams as people first, but what worried me here was whether I could navigate all the complicated issues around people integration in such an emergency situation.

After we built The Wall, there was a temporary uplift in morale because everyone saw the same work being aligned across the teams. But shortly after the work was aligned and execution of the work began, the reality of getting things done tested the team.

We had several obstacles in our way. Some obstacles were political and some were technical, but every one of the obstacles became massive problems in light speed. One very memorable obstacle was about moving the assets from one company to the other in the merger at the "go live" moment. It can be equated to moving furniture from one house to another. But imagine if you were restricted to moving furniture out of one house and into the new house all within six hours and you all only had access to the same truck. Nothing was simple.

The team immediately became worried that this would be impossible. Now, here's where the skills, experience, and history work came into real life. Everyone had an opinion. Even the team members who weren't responsible for managing the asset move had an opinion. In a project where we only had ninety-seven days to do absolutely everything, it's not good when a problem becomes so public across the team and raises competition. It was almost a feeling of "wow…cool problem!" and absolutely everyone wanted to be part of solving it.

As the leadership team, Lee, Ray and I had a problem on our hands. We wanted to include everyone to be sure we didn't miss any ideas, but we needed all the other work to get done as well.

We also didn't want to leave anyone out or offend anyone with morale being so critical in such an aggressive project. We realized we had no choice. We had to limit the subject matter experts and get the problem solved.

We thought long and hard about how the team worked together and their individual histories and came up with the answer. Five subject matter experts were put in a room and we put one of our team leaders, Angie, in charge of this SWAT team. Angie and the SWAT team battled out every option and then presented their recommendation to the other critical opinion holders on the larger team.

Solving this problem forced the generation of a SWAT team approach and still included others on the larger team when the final review was done. The process also allowed others across the project to see the strengths of Angie and her SWAT team so that when we faced other issues during the "go live" weekend, the talents were already known and trusted. We used the SWAT team approach many times over the ninety-seven days and it always worked well to solve problems in a quick and effective manner.

Handling one crisis after another, I kept watching The Wall and the calendar, worrying if we would still get through the work in time...yet knowing we could. In retrospect, I now see that it was the 150 percent commitment to the mission that got us through it all. As an entire team, and using a SWAT team (divide and conquer) approach, we generated an appreciation by all. The teams felt respected and trusted to solve problems without all having to have it their own way all the time.

I will always remember the feelings and the energy of Project

Knightsbridge. This amazing group of individuals, who were already frazzled and frustrated when I arrived on the project, bonded as a team over those ninety-seven days. We worked days that were twenty hours long, seven days a week. We used caterers and had interns who were coffee runners because we stayed on the job night and day. If we didn't force people to go home and sleep, they wouldn't have. The dedication to the cause was amazing to see.

The team on Project Knightsbridge proved to me that teamwork is not just a notion for books or pie-in-the-sky dreaming. Following the simple principles that if you care enough about people, they will care, too, and giving them what they want—communication, decisions, and structure—really does make a difference.

Chapter 5

STEP FOUR: Stock up on Your Soft Skills

In university, theories are taught and many students are able to regurgitate word-for-word the textbook definition of a concept and can give an example. In the real world, a student of life needs to understand by doing. You don't want to be like a robot learning facts and figures, but you need to understand the problems and the people and how they interrelate. Those who know and understand the people landscape are the ones that succeed.

1. **Embrace the Challenge**
2. **Form the Winning Team**
3. **Be the Leader**
4. **Stock up on the Soft Skills**
5. **Make It Happen**

WHY ARE SOFT SKILLS CRITICAL?

Meeting project deadlines and accomplishing your delivery goals with everyone feeling an equal part of it can in fact be arduous. Many people struggle with how to organize people to do difficult things. Leadership is not magic or secretive. It is a practical approach. It is also a considerate approach. If you take your role as a leader to be more of the one who guides, sets examples, and really likes the team, your job will be much easier. Soft skills are not silly to want to have, foster or display. Soft skills are the finesse of leadership.

The Goal Is to Have a Positive Workplace

Having a positive workplace goes back to something we all look for, which is BALANCE. Operating with a code of ethics brings about balance. We need balance as our foundation, in our personal life and our work life. Take a look at the amount of time and energy that you spend at work. Hopefully you are doing a job that you like and that you get satisfaction from. We spend so much time doing our jobs that it really should be a priority to find a position that suits one's personality and work style. People not only change jobs, they change careers and professions. We need a job that fits us because we humans care about quality of life. We crave a well of a deep, profound sense of satisfaction.

Think about this: If someone asked you where you live, what place would you describe and why? Did you immediately think of your house? Is it because you sleep there? You eat some of your meals there? Is your house anything more than the place where your rent or mortgage bills are sent?

Funny, isn't it? If I ask you where you live, you will rattle off your address without thinking. It is one of those things that you instinctively know, but it's surprisingly slippery business trying to say definitively why.

What if we were to actually loosen that idea a bit, and simply say that where you live is a place where you spend a significant amount of your time on a regular (perhaps daily) basis. On purpose, I said *a* place, not *the* place. That is because I want you to consider the idea that you may have more than one place where you live: your place of work, for example.

Let's ponder it this way: You actually *do* things at your place of work; you emotionally invest and divest of yourself there. The places (note the plural word, "places") that you live should be an environment where you feel reasonably safe and comfortable to be who you want to be. If life is reflected in art, then let your work environment be your canvas. It should be a place where you feel sufficiently free to express yourself, to experiment, to grow and learn. Without a real opportunity for personal growth, you are severely limited in how much internal satisfaction you gain from your work and the same goes for those individuals you lead.

Where you live is everywhere. It is great when we reach the conclusion that we live in the here and now. Some days I live on my computer. Right now, you are living with a good book (a little plug of shameless self-promotion). It is also worthy to take note of what makes you feel *alive*. When you realize what lights you up, what gets your juices flowing, you will want to live there more and more.

We all need new challenges. We thrive on them. We need them to survive. A richer and more fulfilling career comes from challenging yourself and gaining mastery of new techniques. Passion, another important positive emotion, is generated in that tingling excitement that comes from tackling something new or meaningful to you.

So how can you know if you and your team are in balance? Sometimes long hours at work are necessary. Therefore, it is imperative that your job gives you enough gratification so that when times get stressful or require all of your energy, you feel that it is worth it. Well, your team is no different. The same balance you are striving for is the balance they are striving for. Managing how you think about soft skills assists in keeping balance for you and your team.

A Healthy Workplace Means Managing Bad Behavior

There are several other specific reasons to ensure you stock up on your soft skills. In times of trouble or stress for a project, different energies may come into play for you and your team. They aren't all good.

This chapter's toolkit also provides a formula that will help you immunize your team.

- Some Bullying May Take Place
- Negativity and Fear May Hover Over Your Team
- Ego Boxing May Be a New Sport
- Ignorance Could Poison the Team's Energy

Bullying: Recognize and Remove

I would imagine that when many of us think of bullying, we envision the scenario of "meet me after school at 3 o'clock on the playground" with the bully and some kid duking it out, surrounded by a crowd of cheering onlookers. The simple fact of the matter is that bullies are here and don't appear to be a dying breed, so until the bully gets a hold of this book and revises his or her attitude and actions, the people working with them need to learn how to best deal with them.

What you need to do is practice all the concepts detailed here. Even if the bully does not reciprocate, you cannot let yourself get hardened or succumb to the pressure and become the bully type yourself. Force yourself to be respectful of this person. Show appreciation when due; hold your tongue in other cases. Yelling or cursing does not advance your cause. The old adage "Kill them with kindness" applies here. This is not a case of "if you can't beat them, join them." You are in fact trying to persuade the bully to come on over to the team of the good guys.

Bullies rarely give credit, for fear it will lead to a lax atmosphere—which, of course, would lead to less work being done and ultimately ruin his or her chances of getting promoted. The selfish bully is really a fearful bully—hesitant and afraid, but afraid to show vulnerabilities. The secret is that we are all vulnerable.

It has been my experience that bullies do not really have their hearts in it. They just don't know of any other way to handle their own insecurities or frustrations. For many of them, it is sometimes almost as stressful to dish it out as to take it.

The point is, if the culture were to change to one where bullying is not tolerated, they would (gladly, I think) change as well. All they need is a little push. Wasn't it Gandhi who said, "Be the change you wish to see in the world"? You can be that change—for this bullying person, for the place you work, for your community, for your family, and for yourself.

There is a distinction between bullying out of panic, fear, ignorance or a need to fit in, and bullying out of sheer malice. There are, unfortunately, those who have learned to derive pleasure from bullying others. You may indeed have to face the worst kind of bully—ones who do it out of a deep-seated frustration and resentment. They seem to truly lack a conscience. They're also, at heart, terribly insecure and wounded. Yes, I said wounded. You must remember from watching nature TV shows that the wounded animal is the most fearsome. You must understand that and have empathy.

The typical bully in grade school is someone who doesn't do well at school and feels a deep shame and insecurity about it. He compensates for that insecurity by physically bullying the other kids. He regains a sense of control by instilling fear in those he believes would otherwise make fun of him. In the workplace, that bully may have grown up with those insecurities still rooted but has learned other methods of inflicting misery and keeping control.

If you don't have your own stories about bully conflicts, I bet you know folks that do. There is the oft-told wisdom that if you just stand up to a bully, they will back down and leave you alone. That tactic is usually futile in dealing with this sort in a workplace situation. You must not underestimate their capacity and willingness for deceit. Do not try to engage in the same kind of manipulation that they employ even if you feel highly justified in doing so. Do not be sucked into their mentality. Take the high road. You will never regret it.

Negativity: Don't Let This Hover Over Your Team

Again referencing *Apollo 13*, the lead pilot said the following about another mission where life and death were in the balance. "You never know what events are going to transpire to get you home." People on or around your team may not have this wisdom and if there is a problem that the team is encountering, the first reaction will be to act negatively and have no faith, only because they are afraid.

Fear is an instinctive part of human nature. If you can understand that the objection you are facing is not personal, not an attack against you, but instead an innate fear of ideas that came from somewhere else, someplace other than their own heads, you will have an easier time dealing with the team. That interloping idea can be seen as an enemy, which, if allowed in, will somehow take over some small part of "me," the mighty ego.

And if you as the leader harbor that same fear, you need to face up to it right now. That sensitivity needs to be dialed down. It really is counter-productive and not good for the health of the team. Try envisioning yourself as a focusing lens or transformative agent. You're trusting in your ability to take an issue or a strategy and own it. When you recommend the solution or direction, there will be negativity among many but the ultimate question to yourself is: What is the right thing to do?

You must also rely on your team's ideas. This will also support avoiding negativity, as they will feel ownership. Working with other ideas is just that—analyzing, understanding and shaping them to fit the context of your particular team's need or problem in your project. By adding your unique perspective and vision to it, you have a hand in the solution. The problem or issue gets ironed out and everyone's ego can feel strong and worthwhile. It is teamwork, after all. The key to remember is that much of people's objections are rooted in fear. Do not block potential progress by fearing it yourself or letting fear take hold of your team.

Many people are working in fear, most often a fear of losing their job. We don't want people to work in fear. As the leader, you need to foster an environment of trust and openness. Being transparent and open in all you do will open the door for the same behavior in return. If you are fearful and obstinate, you cannot expect your team to behave any differently. Take a deep breath and be ready for change. Embrace it!

My one-word piece of advice for you: Persevere. I don't advocate being Pollyanna or Suzy Sunshine. Don't be fake. You can be realistic about the situation and still remain positive. Your positive attitude, your "we can do this together" attitude, will eventually sink in to those around you. It takes time. You cannot cave in to the negativity that you will inevitably face. Every negative remark or action takes three positives to counteract. You must be the face and voice of positivity.

And you know what? There may be some days early on when it may feel like you are the only one with anything positive to say. Don't give in. You have to be the one leading by example. Do what it takes for you to remain positive.

Ego Boxing: This Is Not a Sport You Want Tickets To

The team will work together through all only if they believe they are doing it for the goal, and not for someone's badge to wear as they climb the corporate ladder.

We cannot have a discussion of human nature without mentioning that little three-letter word that can create a great big mess of trouble: the ego.

The ego is a mighty thing. We need it, but sometimes it gets, shall we say, a little carried away. It is amazing how something can be so precious and delicate, yet so powerful and our driving force.

We can all think of examples of ego run amok: at home, at work, in school. You name it. I would love to flat-out say: NO

EGOS ALLOWED, but that is not realistic. The ego is alive and well in every one of us. We can't bar it completely; we need to learn how to live with the ego.

Sometimes the hardest thing to do in the workplace, in the family, or in any community organization is to keep the ego in check. We want to make known our grand ideas and our great thinking skills. Some of us may fall into the "show off" classification. Others are big-talking braggers. Some people have egos so sensitive that they take everything as deep criticism.

As a leader, you have to develop thick skin and leave your ego in your briefcase. If we refer back to the passage from the beginning of the book about climbing the corporate ladder, we will remember to stop and think about what success is and what it means to us. Remember, the personal ladder is much more important.

To get things done, the team as a whole must absolutely trust their leader. If the leader is working in any way under a hero complex, then he or she tends to make decisions to impress, and not to complete the mission. It's true that sometimes this actually doesn't interfere with the ability to complete the task, but when the mission is complex and stressful, this will be the one area that will definitely result in an inability to lead.

Ignorance: This Shows Itself Through Stubbornness

Another segment of ego boxing is the mentality of being set in our ways and not wanting to try something new. Ignorance is primarily the reason for this. I have seen many companies, community organizations and individuals infected with the NIH syndrome. What is NIH? Not Invented Here. The ego wants to take credit for everything, and making use of another's idea is a hard pill for many to swallow. Stubborn individuals want to cut down the idea and point out its flaws. Why? Simply because the idea did not come from them.

It is so much more productive to review the idea, wherever the idea originated, to decide if it has real potential to fill a need or to cure an existing ail, or maybe determine if the idea, method or procedure needs to be tweaked for the needs of this project. The important thing is to be aware that good ideas can come from anywhere. As a good leader, you are open to new ideas. You look for ideas to come from your team. You nurture the seeds that can create new ideas that develop from those around you. Having confidence as a leader means that you can trust others to come up with solutions and you will be glad to welcome and implement those answers.

The sister syndrome to the NIH (Not Invented Here) malady is the NTH syndrome. The Not Thought Here disease is running rampant across every continent on our planet.

People are creatures of habit, there is no doubt about that, but keeping an open mind and being able to consider change, including a slight variation to the tried and true plan, is forward-thinking and what is needed to succeed in the times we live in now.

It is like a weed that is hard to keep out. The pervasive attitude of "but we have always done it this way" is difficult to overcome. It takes time to convince people to try on new ideas.

Sometimes they are not convinced until the end result is achieved and they will then grudgingly concede that yeah, maybe I guess that worked out okay.

ADD TO YOUR LEADERSHIP TOOLKIT:

1. **Embrace the Challenge Using the 3 Cs**
2. **Form the Winning Team With DEUCES**
3. **Be the Leader by Mastering the Art of Leadership**
4. **Stock up on the Soft Skills With the 4 Ls**
5. **Make It Happen With a Secret Formula**

THE 4 LS

When you are at the onset of leading a team of new individuals or already known individuals, the same rules apply. For the lack of a more clever acronym, I will call these tools the 4 Ls: Look, Listen, Learn, and then Lead. Having the 4 Ls in your toolkit will help you embrace any challenge with confidence and clarity.

LOOK

And I mean really look.

Many of us are often quick to judge. With people, we sometimes take a cursory look and instantly make up our minds about a person or the state of affairs. First impressions do matter, don't get me wrong, but most of the time we need to withhold our judgment until we have done more than take a first initial glance. In fact, we would all be better off if we could withhold our judgment, period.

Information-gathering and judging are two entirely different things. Contrary to popular commercials, image is not everything. A "persona" with no person is useless. Life is not form over substance. We want and need the whole person, not just a pleasing outer wrapping.

When you meet your team, look at each person. Make eye contact. Associate the name with the face. See each person for who they are, an individual who wants to do his or her best to make this project a success. As the leader, you will want to do your best to help each team member achieve their goals, which of course also results in a successful project delivery.

Look at the Work the Team Completed So Far

When you take on a new project that is already underway and facing challenges, it may be easy to write off the team's previous achievements because they are currently facing problems. Any previous achievements must be validated, and the team will be more supportive when you want to make changes if you have reviewed and celebrated their previous successes.

Many teams also struggle due to the lack of leadership prior to your arrival on the scene. This would have played into why they are facing challenges. Look for the reason they are struggling and don't guess. Part of the work that you will have reviewed with them when you ASKED them their views will provide you with clues as well.

Validating the team's achievements is excellent and necessary, and you will see a marked improvement in the team's support for your leadership. You will need this support when you review with them the weaknesses in the team strategy and what impacted the team's ability to be completely successful.

All of us should be willing to hear criticism if we know that the positive aspects of what we have done are seen, appreciated, and supported.

LISTEN

We've all heard the phrase "think outside the box." It's a bit overused actually, but leaders need to learn how to listen outside of the box as well. Listening is one of the most taken for granted skills in our modern world. We might hear someone, but we have to tune in to actually listen. It's a mutual benefit. An employee who feels that he is listened to feels valued. That is an intrinsic human need and leaders know to pay attention to what people have to say.

Think about our family lives. We get frustrated when our spouse or children seem to not be listening to us. When a teacher wants the attention of the class, the phrase often uttered is "Listen up." Switch from simply the ears taking in noise to the brain taking in information. Listening is a cognitive function.

Listening Through Open and Transparent Communication

All of the individuals involved must know that, as a leader, you will listen to the issues and concerns no matter how large or small. If the team knows that open and transparent communication is fostered, and that they are listened to, then they are also more likely to express the problems that they are facing with the project in the calm times and the most challenging times as well. In difficult times, leaders cannot pretend that the situation is all sunshine and roses when the team can feel that the project is starting to be like the Titanic headed for the iceberg. Communication means telling the truth.

Teams that are taking on immense amounts of work and spending intense amounts of time together suffer immeasurably from lack of honest and open communication. From day one, I want to foster a spirit of openness. No secrets and no lies—not from me, not from the team, and not from the client.

So I start off by opening it up: "Tell me what's on your mind. What's working and what's not working? I will do whatever I can to fix it." The first day of this open dialogue can be hell in a project in crisis, or even a project in the mobilization stage. There are some people who need to unload every gripe and negative vibe. And they lay it on. And on. And on. And I go home drained.

The second day is hell, too. Most people have had their say, but there are some who have more on their minds. They need to talk. Every day it gets a little better. Now that there is an outlet for their issues, you will also start to get the general complaints, but eventually they'll stop complaining about every little thing and begin to focus on what really needs to be focused on. The important thing is that each person is heard. In any relationship, we all need to be heard. I must stress this point: Give the team the chance to be heard. When someone feels that they are finally being listened to, it makes a drastic improvement in attitude and disposition for the entire team.

Once individuals know they are being heard, they now need to be guaranteed that action follows. If an issue brought up is something that I can resolve, I resolve it immediately. If it takes time, I will say so but I work tirelessly to resolve every single issue…that is my job.

An open and responsive communication approach is also a way that I can get to know the people on the team and they can learn that I am a person of action. This is also the beginning of trust. The team has to get to know me as well, and I have to earn their trust. By inviting communication, I learn what personalities are involved and who has what vantage point.

Everywhere I have worked, in North America, in Europe, or in Asia, there is a consistent presence of frustrated people who feel they are not listened to and not communicated with. It does not take a genius to solve this issue, but so many leaders don't take the time or don't feel it is important, yet it is critical.

Listen to your team. Communicate with your team. Take action for your team. The lines of communication must ALWAYS be open no matter how difficult the situation is to discuss. It may not be pretty in the beginning, and, yes, it can be very tiring, but the results are rewarding for all. An exceptional leader listens to their team members even when the opinions differ dramatically.

There is so much more to listening than processing the words floating about. Life is actually easy if everyone discusses their concerns, but you cannot rely on that. You must learn how to decipher more than one language. I don't mean different languages like French, English, German, etc. I mean different *types* of language.

The Language of Speaking

Words matter. What a person says needs to be heard, interpreted and understood. Some folks are articulate speakers; some are not. You need to be a patient listener and let your colleague or family member say what they need to say without interrupting or trying to finish their statement.

The concepts in this book work together. Listening harkens back to respect. Show that individual that you respect their thoughts by listening to their words. Listening does not imply an automatic agreement or even understanding, but it does indicate that you appreciate a willingness to offer an opinion, and that you will give fair consideration to the feedback or concern.

It's also important that you are as clear as possible with your speaking language and realize that you can say the same thing to fifty people and they will all hear you differently. Expect that your team will need to have your constant patience to reiterate things that you may have thought were simple. Each member of your team also needs to understand each other's speaking language as well.

I would like you to try this exercise with your team and you may find that it illustrates the point much better than I can explain it to you:

1. Ask each person on your team to take a standard piece of paper.
2. Tell everyone to close their eyes, and make sure they know they must not speak or open their eyes at any time during the exercise.
3. Tell the group to fold the paper in half and rip the top right corner.
4. Then tell the group to fold the paper in half again and rip the bottom left corner.
5. And again, tell the group to fold the paper in half and rip the top left corner.
6. Once more, tell the team to fold the paper in half and rip the bottom center.
7. Finally, have everyone open their eyes and open up their papers.

Do you see any papers that look the same? No? Why is that? It's simply because everyone is different; everyone hears differently and everyone interprets differently.

This is an excellent exercise to illustrate to your team that they themselves won't always communicate or speak in a clear enough way to ensure that the instructions lead to the same result. That is why they must focus on being clear and patient when they speak, and now they can understand when other team members don't follow through as expected.

Recognize and Understand the Personal Aspects of Language

In a group meeting, you call people to agreement, and you assume that silence is consent and understanding. What did we say earlier about the word "assume"? Not a good idea. Look around the room again. If you recognize a puzzled face, invite the person to speak. "Hey, Sally, you have a look there—are you concerned?" You need to also recognize that not everyone will feel comfortable speaking up in public. Take note of who expresses questions or concerns in their faces and follow up one-on-one after the meeting.

Just as we cannot judge a book by its cover, or a person by their looks, we need to look beyond the words exchanged and focus on another type of language. Personal language is what many people refer to as body language. The words are just one factor in the whole equation.

The sentence, "Yeah, sure, I can have that done by tomorrow," can mean two entirely different things based on personal language. An eager smile and nod can accompany those words uttered in sincerity. A rolling of the eyes, a crossing of the arms, and a sarcastic tone when saying that sentence means the opposite of the literal spoken language. What that employee is really saying is: You're crazy if you think I can have that done by tomorrow.

Facial expressions and tone of voice go a long way in the understanding of what a person really means. Many relationship experts maintain that personal language is the most important facet of language to gauge someone's true feelings. The point I'm making is that you need to listen intently with your eyes and your ears. Be engaged in the conversation so you do not miss subtle clues.

Be on the Lookout for Absent Language

There may be someone on your team who says nothing when you are all together. Maybe you want to think that because they do not speak up, they are content. Many times that is not the case. There may be some folks that are simply shy, but sometimes there is a person who sits through a meeting stone silent and then outside the conference room has lots to say, all negative.

A good leader is aware that silence is not golden or an indicator that all is well. Maybe some people on the team hold back their comments because they feel that it is pointless to say anything based on past history, when no one cared. There are also times when they are feeling that the group may chastise them for their opinion. Either way, you need to see it and reach out offline with any of these individuals casually to see what their opinions are and how they think. You want the people on your teams to know that their opinions matter and that voicing their opinions is encouraged and valued. That is why I open the lines of communication from the very first day together.

The Way We Type Says What We Mean...
Even When We Don't

Email is a double-edged sword. It is a wonderful technology that provides us the means to now talk to anyone in the world. However, we sometimes use it instead of picking up the phone and calling a person in our own building or even across the hall. Sometimes meanings can be misconstrued in an email. Sometimes people say things in email that they would never say in person. You may know co-workers who are very lovely in person, but when they get back to their computer, they create havoc with their emails. Email has a unique power to alienate.

As a leader, you need to be aware of who is quietly typing negativity throughout the organization. The "reply to all" feature must be used with care. Some people send their complaints for all to see, and that does very little to rectify the situation. It creates a "gotcha" mentality.

If you have an issue with a team member, talk to him or her in person or on the phone. If you must email, be sure to send it only to that person and not broadcast it companywide. Your colleagues need to know that they can trust you, and abuse of email is one sure way to achieve discredit and disaster.

Be very diligent as well to watch for and manage the individuals who have a tendency to use email as a weapon and call them on it. You may find that that person may not have ever had anyone raise it to them and they will be embarrassed, but then they will fix it. Anyone who is hiding behind a computer due to their own insecurities or tendency to bully will require more support and coaching by you, so don't be shy. They will be better off for your coaching on the subject.

LEARN

Learn About the People—Academia With People: Peopledemia

Academia. When you hear that word, you probably think professors, scholars, textbook learning, and the academic life. Academia is fundamental in our lives, as we need a proper education to prepare for our careers, but we also need to look beyond academics. Since the study of science and the arts is referred to as academia, I've thought for years that there should be equal importance on the study of people, hence a new term: peopledemia.

Peopledemia is a term I created that is meant to be an all-encompassing mindset for those in positions of leadership. Before you can lead a team or group of people to deliver on a mission or complete a difficult task, you must take time to study how each person thinks, works, and is motivated, and then your approach in leading teams will foster the right culture.

If we could recognize in our work the cues of our team members and colleagues, we could avoid wasted time due to misunderstandings and low morale issues. Peopledemia is critical to understanding how to be a top-notch leader, especially in a turbulent event. You may be a technical guru and know the technical aspects of what needs to be done to accomplish delivery, but you may be struggling with the leadership aspects of your job. As a leader, you must get every team member involved on working together and know that they are an integral part of the overall success.

To achieve the goal of building a team that can do anything, there are several areas of focus. This specific focus is around learning about your team and each team member by studying their strengths, weaknesses and skills. Peopledemia is the analysis you need for this learning. You will need to figure out each person's approach and thinking and then you must tie that into every combination of the work relationships on your team.

Even in the very simplest of scenarios, it can be complicated. Let's say there is a team of just three people to understand: X, Y and Z. The combinations of relationship lines are X to Y, X to Z and Y to Z. Imagine now multiplying it by five team members; that creates twenty combinations. Imagine a larger workplace with even more team members.

Think of the Rubik's cube. It is in your hands. You are clicking away on each side, twisting and turning around and around to make it complete and correct. Knowing what side goes where and what lines up with what is tricky and takes practice. Think of the dynamics of people like that.

People matter, whether they have ever mastered the Rubik's cube or not. But be encouraged—the melding of minds can lead to the melding of hearts and that's where teamwork really kicks in.

In all honesty, it's all a big puzzle. Your job as the leader is to make the pieces of the project and the people of the project come together. When faced with change, everyone reacts differently. You as the leader need to be able to understand each person's way. That requires time and commitment.

A good leader must be committed to make that effort. You couldn't possibly analyze every combination with a team of hundreds, but you can open your mind to it so that when you need to be involved in sorting out an issue, this approach will help you do so with a positive result. Remember that most issues and problems facing teams are not purely on the technical level—they are from a disconnect between individuals. They are usually due to a lack of understanding, either about the role they play or the objective in front of them.

The end result of applying peopledemia is better than the paycheck. The end result can be a team that comes together and the loyalty lasts forever. You can create a team that can work together forever and tackle whatever comes its way.

Learn About the Work

Of course you know the work if you are the leader, right? Well, not necessarily. You many have worked in the trenches leading up to your new position and believe that you are now in a position where you do not need to get into the detailed work. This is a wrong assumption. It is true that you don't want to do your team's work for them and you also do not want to micro-manage, but you still need to know the work.

Once you have built a top-notch team and put forward your vision, it is critical that you understand the work and constantly remain connected to the work that is being completed. You need to find a balance between extreme delegation and micro-management.

Leaders who stay in their ivory tower mentality will eventually become out of touch. I like to be with the troops as much as possible by literally sitting beside a testing expert and having them teach me the tests they are running and the system that we are building. I love to be with the team when they run their first major test on a new system that will be launched to hundreds of clients.

I have even pretended to be the user of an application at the time it is ready for testing and have the team teach me the application from start to finish. You are never "above" the work. An effective leader understands what needs to be done and integrates with their team in a way that is not overbearing, but supportive.

The team appreciates a leader who takes the time to learn the work and you will benefit from this, the team will benefit from your involvement, and the project will ultimately benefit as well. "Being there" is not just a catch phrase. It's an important approach and practical application of leadership.

Learn About Each Other's Roles in the Mission

At the beginning of every new department I'm building or project I'm running, I take as many of the team offsite as possible and we do a couple of things. We learn about the mission in more detail, we learn about the expectations of the external influencers, and we build a culture.

Any first-time team that I take offsite for a strategy work session is first put through an exercise that involves playing with Tinker Toys. I try to find the traditional wooden Tinker Toys instead of the plastic ones to make it more authentic. The goal of this exercise is to teach teams and team members how to relate to each other around role definition and completion of a project. I have used this exercise to teach MBA students about how important it is to learn each other's job. A great deal of my experience comes from projects that were building large computer systems, and with large systems development projects something needs to be built and eventually installed with a client for their use in everyday business processing.

For purposes of explaining this exercise, I will use systems development roles, but you can customize the exercise to meet your specific role types for your project or mission. In systems development, there are five key roles at the core: one, the end user; two, the systems architect; three, the programmer; four, the systems tester; and five, the project manager.

Now do the following (let's say that your team is fifty people):

1. Take a hat and put in fifty small pieces of folded paper with each role written on them (ten with "programmer," for instance).

2. Pass the hat around to each member of your team. Ask one person to begin. Each person pulls a paper out of the hat. After a few minutes, everyone will have selected a role.

3. Ask each project manager to find their end user,

systems architect, programmer and systems tester and form their team. Just for fun, they should name their team as well.

4. Now, get out a box of Tinker Toys for each team. With Tinker Toys, you can build anything, right?

5. Tell the end user to pick what they want the team to build for them.

6. Instruct each project manager to take ten minutes and have everyone understand their roles on their team.

7. Instruct the end user to keep the team honest with the end objective and not give in to change.

8. Give everyone thirty minutes to get the job done and remind them that they all must play their own roles, whichever one they drew out of the hat.

So now the team is bonding and building. Remind them that they must use every piece.

An even more interesting twist on the rules is that the project manager can negotiate with other teams to exchange parts to complete their mission. This allows for all ten teams to rely on each other.

When every team has made it through the thirty-minute exercise, it will be clear and they will have had a great time. Now, each end user (or client, as they are sometimes referred to) must present to the entire team what the goal was and how the team delivered on that goal, and the lead developer must demonstrate the product.

I use this exercise to bring a new team together and as part of a full-day planning session. It breaks the ice for the day and creates camaraderie for all as well. In addition, I put a piece of colored paper under one chair at each table so that when we finish the exercise, the person sitting in the chair with the colored paper can take the creation home to their families. I now use this exercise in every project with every team because a) it's fun b) it gets people who haven't met to know each other and c) it takes people out of their comfort zone in a fun environment to begin to understand each others' roles.

We are used to doing what we do, our own little piece of the pie, and we often want to point the finger of blame toward everyone else when a project falls into crisis mode. By learning what the other team roles are, it is easier to understand the overall complexity of a project and to appreciate all the other pieces of the puzzle. If we take the time to learn and care about each other's roles, the entire project becomes more cohesive and fluid, and there is an increased atmosphere of trust and cooperation.

LEAD

Look, listen, learn. The end result is being able to lead. The more you inherently believe that people matter, the more this becomes second nature. Assume that a situation arises and you are needed to provide leadership. You can take stock of the language (all of them) and the situation, and look to see the individuals' reactions. To lead with the right level of integrity, two golden rules should be observed. One, make personal commitments part of your leadership approach and two, make professional commitments part of your leadership approach.

The reason for embracing these golden rules is that in the twenty-first century, there is a great deal going on in everyone's lives and everyone is trying to get things done and still do the right thing. These two rules will help alleviate stresses, avoid little problems turning into big problems, and help you make it happen.

There will still be emotionally charged moments in your project, but if you work very hard to align the needs of the team with the goals that they have to meet, then making it happen will be much easier.

Golden Rule #1: Make Personal Commitments Part of Your Leadership Approach

How your team and your colleagues perceive you is important and is something that you should care about. Your ability to deliver results with a team that will work hard to make anything happen requires you to be authentic in your approach.

Personal commitments to yourself about how you interact with others and how you evolve as a leader will also give you a better result in your everyday management style. There are two categories of personal commitments that you should evaluate in yourself and strive to maintain or improve: personal inward commitments and personal outward commitments.

Personal inward commitments are those you make to yourself

that will enable you to attain higher goals. You will reach for goals that are beyond your comfort zone and you will do it knowing you have a great chance to succeed.

1. ***Trade the corporate ladder for the your personal leadership ladder:***
   There is no need to manage your goals against a corporate ladder mentality if you deliver results. If we stay on the ladder image, think about each rung being the same. Turn that ladder sideways or upside down and each rung is still the same. We use the ladder to go up and down to take care of what we need to do. Sometimes we do indeed lay it on its side and use it as scaffolding. The rung in the middle is just as important, just as strong, and as very much needed as any other rung. So doesn't it make sense that we should treat all rungs the same? When you use my delivery methodology to make things happen, you are using the ladder as your own personal leadership ladder.

2. ***Take pride in yourself as a leader:***
   The first step in the process is to take pride in you. You as the leader must care about your ability to lead and you must care about each individual on your team. Think of a student in school. All students want to do well but need the tools and guidance to be able to master the concepts. If they think nobody cares, then they may stop caring, too. The old attitude of

"why bother?" pushes out the pride. It's human nature. We need someone to care.

3. ***Do it well or don't bother:***

    I've heard this concept called the "and then some" principle. It's very simple. Whatever the task at hand is, do it, do it well, and then some. People often ask me how I moved so quickly up the ranks in the business world. Basically, I did what I was asked to do and always a little bit more. I complied with the "and then some" mentality without knowing it. It is just the way I am wired. I want to do a good job. No, I want to do a great job. Even if it is not your inherent nature to automatically do a little bit more, you can train yourself to do so. And mentor your team to adopt the "and then some" principle, too!

4. ***Be dependable:***

    Think about all the people you deal with on a daily basis. Most of us like to work with dependable people. We do so without cognitively assessing the various skills of our co-workers. If something needs to get done, there is always a "go to" person that the others feel assured will get that part of the project done. Being dependable is one of the greatest personality traits you can have. And if you feel you are lacking a little in this department, it's an area that improves with action. Now think for a minute what would happen if you built a team of several of these individuals. Then you have many "go to" people.

That should be the goal of all leaders, building the A-Team.

Dependability is crucial. If ever there were a fundamental in the world of business or working with others, being dependable is the vital factor, the decisive tell-all. If you cannot depend on someone, then there is no trust and it can all fall like a house of cards.

5. *Have balance:*

Balance is key, personally as well as professionally. Keep your family at your center. I have a crazy work life sometimes, but my husband and my kids know that they are priority number one and if someone in the family needs me, I'm there. It's funny how things work; generally things can happen personally when business is calm and then business can have a crisis when the personal life is calm. Each one always needs to know that they matter, too. Be approachable, at work and at home. If your team member or your child needs to talk, you need to have an open-door policy. Be available. Be authentic. Be yourself. It will all fit in.

6 *Don't ever quit:*

Basically, as the leader, all you do every day is help people. That is why I know that we all have leadership potential within each and every one of us. Leadership is a skill that you can master no matter who you are, what you do, or where you come from. You just have to care enough to want to.

The second category is outward personal commitments. These are commitments that you make to yourself that deal with others, including colleagues and your team members. Look at these as personal commitments that set an example for the team. They aren't openly discussed, but they directly affect the spirit of the team. At first, these may look to be commitments that should be added to your professional commitments list, but those are ones that you would also hold your team accountable to in an open conversation. These are more personal.

1. *Always be on top of your game:*
   If you expect the best from your team, then you owe them the same. I liken it to being a singer. If I can't hit that high note, I don't go on stage. I know it is my job to be on my game, to be "up." In order to do so, I must build into my schedule some downtime, some time to regroup and collect myself out of the fray. I usually work from home one day a week. It gives me the opportunity to decompress and it gives the team the chance to solve some problems without me hanging around.

   Recharging the batteries is crucial. The team and the project deserve to have me at my best, and sometimes that means staying away. You know your energy cycle and when you perform best. Adapt your schedule to allow your brain and your physical and mental body to refuel. Don't try to be Superman or Superwoman. Burning the candle at both ends is dangerous. Getting burnt out is counter-productive, and in the end, very damaging for all concerned.

2. ***Practice patience:***
   A good leader practices patience. It may not come easily, but with time and effort, patience can be learned—it is difficult, but it can! Patience means not jumping to conclusions. Patience means not interrupting others. Patience means knowing that an answer will eventually present itself and there is no need to panic.

   One more thing—patience does not mean being a pushover. Sometimes a member of the team, from the very high up "person with the power" to the very opposite end of the spectrum, can test your patience for the very reason of seeing how far they can go. If you are a model of patience, someone might want to test you, to push your buttons to see what it takes to put you over the edge. Do not let yourself get taken advantage of; hold firm, be patient, yes, but when work is due, it's all in the delivery and that's why we are there: to learn how to get it done. You can be patient, but there comes a point when the team has to get it done. It's all in the delivery. If we don't deliver this time, there is no next time.

3. ***Cut the emotion and deal with the facts:***
   Assume there is a problem on the project. (There will always be problems on projects.) The team members are all individuals with differing ways of doing things

and differing ways of reacting. It is your job to learn to read these differing dynamics.

In general, it usually boils down to the fact that most people are worried or scared or unsure about what to do next. No one will come forward and say, "Gee, I feel scared." But you can bet they are feeling a bundle of emotions. You, as leader, need to simply break it down. Acknowledge their fears. Admit that, yes, it is scary. Say something to the effect of "We are facing new territory here and we need to put our minds together to solve this problem." In doing this, you have done something very important, though you may not realize that you have done anything. So what have you done? You have validated their fears and thus validated them. Everyone feels the need for validation.

We humans need to be confirmed in our feelings. We seek validation without knowing it. This allows the team or individuals feeling the stress to now remove the emotion and you can work through the facts of the problem with them without emotion derailing the effort.

4. *Know what you are good at and join forces with people who complement your skills:*
   People—the team and the board and the CEO that hired you—are relying on you. You have to know who you are and you have to know that you are ready. Your only service is to the team and the project. You

need to know who your team is and what the required task is.

5. ***Admit mistakes and lessons learned, and adjust your approach:***
You need to be part of the team, to be involved, so you know who and what is meshing and what is not. It is a constant. As the leader, you have accepted the challenge and you need to care enough to make it happen. If the vision you laid out has flaws or problems, don't be afraid to be open to that. If you discover that the particular path is wrong and does not lead to your end delivery, then do not hesitate to change the path rather than focusing on how it might make you look.

6. ***Show compassion:***
Compassion is the key to bonding as a team. The one thing that I cannot teach you is how to care. I can repeat that you have to care, and it is my firm belief that anyone reading these pages does have a desire for better human connection, interaction, and communication. I thank you.

Some managers, however, think that they don't need to care. They tell themselves that there is someone else in the company that cares and that will work as a substitute for their lack of caring. Not true. Maybe your assistant cares, and that is wonderful, but you as a leader need to show your team members that you care. Caring about them and the project needs to be expressed, but do not overdo it. Remember to strive for balance in all things. Some people may not want a gushy leader, so temper your praise to the individual, but don't skimp on the praise.

7. ***Really listen, don't just pretend:***
I help my team get through the rough times. There will be rough times. There will be problems on the project. There will be personality problems. I am not a psychologist, but I am a good listener and I care. Most of the time, no matter what the problem is, it can be relieved, even if not fully or immediately solved, simply if the person has someone who will truly listen to them and who truly cares.

Golden Rule #2: Make Professional Commitments Part of Your Leadership Approach

1. ***Know that your role is primarily issues resolution:***
Your job is to work every day to help the team solve their problems. There are always problems, some big, some small. Be involved. Know what the problems are and seek answers and advice from your team experts so that you can provide guidance and make critical decisions. If the team is stumped, reach outside of the team and don't stop until a solution is found.

2. ***Lead your team in an open and trustworthy environment:***
I teach trust. The team needs to know that they can trust me. This point cannot be underestimated. They

also need to know to trust each other. I in turn need to know that I can trust them. If I cannot trust someone, I cannot have them on my team.

On every project, I find out about the team. I get to know the dynamics of the individuals. This is a great way for me to get a feel for all the complex personalities and how they relate to each other. It is also good for them to feel me out. Seeds of trust are planted immediately.

3. *Manage expectations:*
   Managing expectations is actually a really cool commitment. If you work hard to manage expectations openly, and train your team to do so as well, when something difficult is facing the team, no one is caught off guard because they were given the heads up. Managing expectations can keep your management, as well as the team, calm through a crisis.

4. *Learn about the work and your team:*
   I ask them to teach me what we need to do. I need to understand the project and the pieces. I will talk to everyone from point A to delivery and ask questions. I am never afraid to ask questions.

   I will ask the entry-level workers how they do their jobs and I will ask the CEO about his or her role. I need to understand what exactly needs to be done. DO NOT shortcut here. Taking the time up front to learn the lay of the land is vital. You may feel the urge to jump and start tackling an issue here or there, but being too hasty only costs time in the long run. Time is our most precious commodity.

5. ***Be a peacekeeper and leader for all and you will succeed:***

As a leader, you have to realize that people are not the means to an end. They are the lifeblood of the project. There can be no delivery without the sustained cooperation of a group of individuals. That is exactly what they are—many pieces who, when put together, are great together.

Every individual is a part of the puzzle, and the puzzle needs each and every single piece, be it a simple ten-piece puzzle or a complex thousand-piece puzzle. To get the desired results, it takes the efforts of all team members to crystallize into the final product, the delivery.

The hardest part of learning to work with people is the attitudinal change that is required. To become an effective leader, you have to learn to view your co-workers as likable aunts, uncles, cousins, all with their own quirky foibles, but also all with capabilities, needs, and dreams. All need to know what direction the company is rowing in and what their part is in getting there. You need to know how to guide them, each in their own unique way, to get them there.

6. ***Don't delegate your vision—empower others to implement it:***

I help finish the project. We all do all the parts and

bits and pieces and I help whomever, wherever, whenever to keep all parts humming along. Notice how often I used the word "help." I am not the master who does it all. I help the team to do it all. A good leader is a good helper. Working side by side, so much more gets done and the camaraderie and the productivity can really soar.

7. *New ideas are good—accept differing opinions:*
People all get their stuff done in their own different ways. You, the leader, have to accept that someone will do something differently from you. There are many ways to do many things. Be open to new possibilities.

8. *Let people shine; don't take leadership credit alone:*
Part of celebrating success is enjoying it with the team. Small successes throughout the project should also be achieved and it's important that all team members know that the individual really accountable for the work—and, as a result, the success—will be given credit where credit is due. This should also be something that you as a leader mandate as part of your culture with the team. All leaders of your support teams must take this on, as it will ensure that people will really want to strive to be the best.

9. *Stay connected:*
To be effective, you have to be there. In the trenches. You have to know what is going on. You don't phone in and demand status reports. You must be aware of

the problems and let the team know that they can count on you to trust them to find their own solutions sometimes. You are not the fairy godmother, the keeper of the magic wand. Each and every team member wields the power.

10. *Every person is equal—they just differentiate in experiences:*

If you currently are in a leadership position, think for a moment how you relate to your employees. Did that sentence even make you blink or give you pause for thought? Do you see the folks that work with you as your employees who work for you, or do you view them as your colleagues and your co-workers?

You may think I am being picky with semantics, but I assure you that how you think affects your actions. The leader is not the person over here and the team the group over there. It is one big group. Even if you technically are "the boss," your manner and attitude pervade your relationships regardless of your word choice. Your "labels" for people, spoken or unspoken, are an indicator of your mindset.

Have you ever overheard someone say, or caught yourself saying, "She's just the secretary" or "He's only an assistant." Many managers fall into this condescending language trap and they don't even realize it. Do you think the secretary or the assistant notices it?

I have a little mental exercise for you. Today, pay attention to how you categorize people. You may think that you do not lump people into one basket or another, and maybe you don't. Pay attention to it and find out for yourself.

This is a simple assignment: From your first interaction with your family in the morning through the entry into your workplace and in your dealings with people during your daily routine, make a conscious effort to recognize your feelings and attitudes toward the different people you encounter throughout your entire day.

How we treat people is such a simple thing, and that's what makes it so easy to overlook. You just need to adjust your attitude and make this new attitude a habit. You may have to check yourself every day. Whom do you dismiss as "unimportant"? Then ask yourself, "How would I feel if the situation were reversed?"

11. *Hold your team accountable:*
    As the team leader, you must hold your people accountable. You, too, must be dependable and set the bar high. It is imperative that the team is able to depend on you and it is critical that you can depend on the team and that they can depend on each other.

12. *Make your company's number one asset its people:*
    It is absolutely crucial that companies see that their number one asset is people. My entire methodology is based on one very simple philosophy: People matter. When considering the basic principles of

human behavior, it becomes clear how to handle any given situation: the Golden Rule. "Do unto others as you would have them do unto you" must always be first and foremost in your mind.

BACK TO DELIVERY

In a corporate document at the completion of Project Knightsbridge, one source stated that the reason he was impressed with me (he did not know me before I showed up that first day) was because when "the dock was burning," I found a way to put out the fire, and in the process, I also kept everyone calm. This was a huge compliment for someone in charge of delivery for a major project. At the onset of the project, though, nothing seemed certain or calm.

We had put up The Wall and although it was far from easy, we did it in just one day. The problem was that not everyone agreed with this approach. The negative feedback began and it started to penetrate the team. When negativity visits, everyone second-guesses the way in which we go about delivering the mission. My vision was questioned because it seemed different than what anyone else was doing on project delivery industry-wide.

So I immediately went into action to solve the concerns and not take it personally. Cut the emotion; deal with the facts. The team needed comfort, not defensiveness. In my mind, it was critical to go to the formula, and although I didn't have it written down then, I knew it instinctively: Create energy around the delivery approach. I was also extremely fortunate that Lee and Ray never wavered on the approach and supported me daily in helping to bring the team along, despite concerns.

I met with the key leaders from each team and gave them a more in-depth view of the reason The Wall would work and why the team should stay with it. I took questions from each leader and they conveyed their concerns to me openly, which was so great but also hard to hear. Some had to do with the newness of the approach, but most actually were just the misunderstanding of it. When problems were raised and ideas provided to improve the approach, I happily adopted change to make things better. Once I spent the time to have open communication, we were back on track within a day.

It would not be fair to leave you with the impression that negativity only visited the team once. This was actually the second time; the first was quite early in the game, and there are several examples that I have no room in this book to tell you about. Some individuals tied to the problems that were facing the project as we arrived on the scene said to my two colleagues and me, "You'll never get everybody to work together. It can't be done." Gee, thanks a bunch. What a counterproductive statement. It actually is sort of comical: "Thanks for coming here to help, but I really don't think you can do it. It can't be done."

The world is full of people who feel that way. How many times have you heard someone say, "It can't be done"? I've faced that a lot in my career, and in the end, they come around. Little by little, one by one, we can change that mentality. Don't ever believe it when someone tells you that you'll never do it. I don't care what the "it" is—you can indeed make it happen.

This Project Knightsbridge was, to put it mildly, a big mess. It was the most challenging project that I had ever tackled up until that point, and although I've dealt with more difficult since, it is my favorite project. As they say, the bigger the challenge, the sweeter the success. For me, Project Knightsbridge was the first full-scale, expected-to-fail project that I had been expected to turn around, and everything that happened throughout the course of the project embodies my whole philosophy. All these principles here were applied, and they worked.

I had only been with this new firm six months so by being the "new kid," the newcomer to the situation, I may have been at a disadvantage, but I see it as an advantage. I saw the situation with new eyes. I was not bogged down with what had already happened. I saw where the project had been and where it needed to go, and I tried to cut through all the emotion, all the history, all the B.S., and just lay it all out there.

In the beginning, every project seems overwhelming. I have those initial moments of "what have I gotten myself into?" but then the calm returns. I remind myself that I have been through this before. I remind myself of Project Knightsbridge and the lessons I learned that formalized my approach to getting things done.

On Project Knightsbridge, I got to know the team and I worked tirelessly to motivate them and give them the energy to succeed. I faced a challenge that I never expected right near the end of our mission. It truly tested my ability to see my commitment to the team through to the end.

As I have attempted to illustrate, several important skills are needed to ensure that the team is motivated and energized, but those are also the skills needed to manage panic and fear from outside and within the team.

The Project Knightsbridge objectives were extremely difficult and the technology logistics very risky, as I've stated throughout the story, and the shortened timeframe added to the risk. Well, nearing the ninety-day mark and the "go live" moment, several aspects of the risks were starting to worry the leadership of the firm back in New York. This became the largest challenge to deal with of all my challenges in the project.

It had only been ninety days, but I knew this team, heart and soul. There came a situation where I had to believe in them, like they believed in me, and put it all on the line.

In the movie Apollo 13, the team in Houston had done everything possible to get the crew ready to re-enter the atmosphere and everyone knew that they only had a slight chance for success. It was explained as being like a baseball thrown from fourteen feet to a target as wide as a piece of paper.

In Project Knightsbridge, our challenge wasn't life or death and it sure wasn't in that range of success. We had much better chances, which is why when the moment came to give the thumbs up for "go live," I was shocked to see such opposition.

The management team from New York landed on U.K. soil to be sure the team was ready to make this complicated mission succeed during what would be a very risky and complicated "go live." They knew how incredibly complicated the implementation was that we were testing and practicing weekend after weekend, and they were worried. That negativity and concern was not shared by the troops. Everyone had worked day in and day out for ninety-plus days to meet this objective. The team was ready.

In *Apollo 13*, the mission control leader heard negativity and concern in the background and turned to them to say, "With all due respect, sir, I believe this is going to be our finest hour." And it was.

In my case, I was a bit more dramatic. Let's just say that I could have taken my own advice on how to influence others through calm and concise communication. Instead, I passionately argued our case and pleaded for the executive team not to lose faith in our team. "We are ready! Give us the GO!"

The room was full of top executives and everyone agreed to sleep on it. Ryan, Lee and I pulled our fearless leader, Marty, into a room and pleaded the case again. At one point, the three of us were clearly ganging up on Marty, and to his credit, he didn't run away.

Later, people would remember that night of pleading our case in funny stories that at the time weren't funny—but after we delivered the results, the scenario seemed funny and will for all time. That one day actually bonded all stakeholders together. Mission control with the president's office, if you will.

I had never been more frightened to take a stance, but also never so proud to take a stand. The team could do it and I knew it; I just had to convince the upper powers of that fact. To me, it was fact. I had spent the time with the teams, knew the individuals, and knew the sacrifice and the quality of their work. I knew enough to know that my convictions were backed up!

The next day we got the green light. All of the work had paid off—we got the GO and we weren't afraid; we were prepared!

Chapter 6

STEP FIVE:
Make It Happen!

Throughout the first four steps, I have specifically talked about how to use your professional tools, and did not try to educate readers on technical methodologies. The goal was to enhance your professional skills with some tried and true methods to provide you with a new methodology for getting things done while caring for the people on your team.

Now it's time to pull it all together. In normal times, the lessons themselves say enough, but what about pulling a rabbit out of a hat? Facing tough times in any initiative is when the leaders really need to know how to pull it all together. You must now take the key aspects of the five steps and use them to achieve anything!

1. **Embrace the Challenge**
2. **Form the Winning Team**
3. **Be the Leader**
4. **Stock up on the Soft Skills**
5. **Make It Happen**

We have discussed throughout these steps the importance of the team and your leadership approach with that team. There are some benefits to the approaches discussed where your career is concerned as well. When you make things happen, you succeed at your chosen profession.

As a results-oriented individual, you take things on so that you can see a mission to completion and you like the challenges that it may bring. It's great to see the team meet the objectives and see the fireworks display upon successful completion. Think of fireworks as an analogy. They require a complex mix of ingredients. Each ingredient is unique and necessary, but each one on its own doesn't really do much. When combined together in the right mix, they create magic. When the "go live" date hits for those ingredients, when that fuse is lit, the pieces are working together for a stunning, magnificent display that literally takes our breath away.

I think about all the projects that I have worked on, including Project Knightsbridge, and I realize that the fireworks happened because I applied the same principles every time but was careful to customize my approach to the needs of the specific project and the new team. When the "go live" date comes, we do it. We light the fuse and let the fireworks happen.

ADD TO YOUR LEADERSHIP TOOLKIT: A SECRET FORMULA

People don't want to be seen as interchangeable parts. Each person is an individual and needs to be treated as such. The bottom line is that people want to be inspired. They want to work at a place that they can believe in. It may sound oversimplified, but if you believe in your employees, they will believe in you and in themselves.

1. **Embrace the Challenge Using the 3 Cs**
2. **Form the Winning Team With DEUCES**
3. **Be the Leader by Mastering the Art of Leadership**
4. **Stock up on the Soft Skills with the 4 Ls**
5. **Make It Happen With a Secret Formula**

We sometimes struggle with how to lead teams through unchartered waters and know that we will succeed. I was looking at my toolkit for helping out with this problem and saw that the acronym was very similar to Einstein's theory of relativity. Then I did a bit of research on his theory.

On the surface, $E=mc^2$ seems very straightforward, but I found it interesting that what Einstein was doing was joining together what was previously thought of as two different concepts, space and time. He joined these two together and proved that, provided with a certain amount of mass, one could calculate the amount of energy it contains and vice versa.

Well, with managing the personal aspects of leadership, you need to generate energy, but with motivation, communication and congratulation. Also, you can actually calculate the level of energy you can get from your team members if you know their amount of motivation, communication and commitment to congratulations. So, my personal take on the formula for creating energy is a bit different:

$$ENERGY\ EQUALS$$
$$MOTIVATE,\ COMMUNICATE\ AND\ CONGRATULATE!$$
$$E = m2c$$

The First Ingredient: Motivate

Each person on the team needs an inner drive to carry out tasks in his or her respective realm, in order for the group as a whole to drive the project on to completion. Morale and motivation are closely intertwined and generate the energy that your team needs to accomplish anything. Morale is a universal model. A company, a family, or a committee all suffer or succeed depending upon low or high morale. When the goal seems unachievable, it is the leader that must motivate the team not to give up.

The word "*team*" is of course used throughout the book, but I want to stay away from the rut of the "teamwork rah-rah," "there's no I in team," "are you a team player?" and all the worn-out expressions you've already heard. I want you to learn how to really work with others, and how to bring out the best in other people. It can be that simple.

An effective leader can still be demanding but fair by exhibiting soft skills. Think of an athletic trainer. You wouldn't expect that person to just sit back and applaud your efforts, whether you do a little, a lot or nothing at all. The trainer is sort of "in your face," but in a positive way. I'm extremely fortunate to have one of these trainers. Sandra is very focused and direct, but is always encouraging me all along the way and pushing me to do more but also doesn't let me get away with being a wimp. I'm pushed, but not ordered. I'm motivated and not made to feel badly if I don't achieve. It makes me want to work harder, not less! As a trainer works with athletes, a good leader works the team to their edge, motivates them, keeps them positive, and keeps them focused on the end result.

One more thing a leader needs to do is just as important as the other steps along the way, and that is to celebrate wins. Success should always be celebrated.

Imagine you have been working with a personal trainer who has motivated you to run a race. At the finish line, you expect a congratulations from this person who has helped you achieve this goal. If he simply said, "Great. Now let's get to work on the next one," you would feel deflated and not motivated to continue on with him or your training. You need to celebrate milestones and accomplishments along the way, to let off steam, plus, of course, mark the big delivery at the end of the project. Team spirit is not just a high school concept. Camaraderie among co-workers makes for a fulfilling and productive work environment. Shared success is often more fulfilling than a solo accomplishment.

Leading Through Orders Is not Motivating

Order is required for a great team, but ordering is not. When you have looked, listened and then learned about your team as individuals—and then as a team—you truly need to apply what you have discovered. When you as leader become embroiled in solving conflicts or motivating through turbulent times, the knowledge you have of your team will help guide you on how to handle them and the situation at hand.

There is the old saying, "You can lead a horse to water but you can't make it drink." Dealing with a team in crisis can seem the same way. However, if you have spent time learning the 4 Ls of your team, you can lead them to water and lead them to drink if that is what is needed. Each team member may need to be led in a different way. You will know that because you have invested your time in the team and what makes each individual tick. This is an important tool to be used whenever you need it.

Keeping Your Cool Will Motivate
Through Hard Times

The path to leadership is not pointing fingers, pounding on desks, or beating on your chest. The hallmark of a good leader is the person who can be the calm in the storm, the one to say, "Okay, let's think things out. There is a solution and we will find it."

Now, it's important to know that I struggle as well with striving for perfection in my leadership style. No one is perfect.

There are days that I don't live up to my own goals; I stop and feel bad, and then I commit that I will do better. That's all this is…your team should know that you aren't perfect, either. It's about going for 150 percent. Sometimes you achieve 100 percent and sometimes you may only get ninety percent.

Some people are easier to deal with than others. The gripers and moaners and pessimists may want to shoot you down. Learning to tactfully deal with negatives is part of the process. When you live your life with ethics and integrity and treat others as you want to be treated, you are already achieving anger management skills and people management skills.

Yes, there will be times when you get angry. How you handle your emotions is indicative of the type of leader you can be. Strive to not ever lose your temper. Lose your temper and you lose your team. Maybe understanding the psychology of a temper might help you put it in check, if you have one. I've come up with this one:

TEMPER = <u>T</u>o be <u>E</u>gotistical, <u>M</u>ad, <u>P</u>aranoid, <u>E</u>nvious and <u>R</u>idiculous

One of my cardinal rules is no yelling. Shouting at people only serves to undermine your credibility and any authority that you have established. Being a blowhard boss who bellows at people is a stereotype that we don't want to perpetuate. Good leaders should be emulated, but perhaps the only way your behavior would be imitated in that scene is for others to be mocking you behind your back.

For some people, keeping emotions in check comes naturally. For others, it will require a little restraint and a little practice. You do not have to give up stating your opinions; it is how you state them that matters.

Tone of voice can turn off a person and they won't listen to a word you're saying. The tone you use can be just as belittling as your actual word choice, and I struggle at times with this as well. There are many times personally and professionally when I can point to my own approach in a stressful situation and I'm less than proud of how I reacted. We all have those moments and what we need to remember is that a bad reaction is not what makes us who we are—and that we just need to strive to improve the next time.

A Happy Employee Is a First-Class Employee

I'm sure you've all heard the line, "A happy wife means a happy life" for husbands to recite daily. I often chuckle at it because I actually think a happy husband means a happy life, too...but it doesn't rhyme. Well, at work, I am all about happiness, too. Being happy boils down to having joy in the everyday things. If you don't find joy in your work, go find something else to do. Blunt, maybe, but when all is said and done, there are really just two important questions in life:

Did you find joy in your life? Did your life bring joy to others? Joy. Simple, profound, wonderful joy. Joy starts from within. You can radiate joy by being true to yourself. Always, always, always be yourself. Strive to be the best person and worker you can be, and you will find joy. And when you get turned on, lit up, excited with joy, you will want to share it with others. People will want to work with you because you are a joy to be around.

Think about it. Work is a major part of our life. Don't you think that we should find joy in our work? My best advice is to love what you do. Find your passion. Don't follow the path of least resistance. Don't succumb to the negativity surrounding you. You can find joy in whatever you do.

Make an Attractive Place to Work

The number one reason that people are motivated to work is because they care. They care about pride in their own work, they care about their team, and they care about the project at hand. Most people inherently want to do a good job. We all want to succeed. You have to give your team the tools to let them succeed.

It is often said that in relationships, opposites attract. That may be so. But in the work environment, like attracts like. Your company, your project, whatever it may be, is only as good as the skill and dedication of the staff. You want top-notch people? Yes, you can hire them, but the real trick is to retain them. Keeping great people is a sign of a great leader. People will flock to a caring leader and head for the hills from an overbearing boss.

Great employees build great companies and vice versa. You want, and need, a work culture that fosters success. The icing on the cake is a dedicated team of workers at all levels and positions of the company. The puzzle is not complete without all the pieces.

When I talk about motivating a team, I mean it in the very best and purest sense of the word. It is not my style to spew all the latest buzzwords at you or to create hype in an effort to whip the team into a frenzy of pumped-up energy. You know the kind of rhetoric that I'm referring to—the pep talk before the big game, the politician's rah-rah speech, or the company bigwigs putting on a song and dance show to get the workforce fired up. There's nothing wrong with that tactic; it is just not what I like to do. Creating a circus is only a temporary measure. Eventually the tents get packed up and the elephants are marched off. I want to create a lasting, trusting atmosphere that is motivating, but not a carnival.

Whatever your position or situation, you can become the focal lens sparking a positive chain reaction toward organizational growth and personal growth. You can create a place where people and ideas flourish. You can create a place where future leaders are challenged and nurtured. You can create it and in doing so you create a force of motivation, in yourself and in those around you.

Have you ever had a schoolteacher or professor who you really liked? They seemed to honestly care about your progression. I'm willing to bet you worked a little (or a lot) harder for that person because you did not want to let them down. They did a simple act of caring and it was a motivating factor.

From what I have witnessed in many companies, management does not, by and large, seem to understand that they can have this very same effect on their staff. Sometimes we make things harder than they have to be. Letting people know that you care is so simple yet so significant. It can have a colossal impact on people and a program and a project.

That is what I see on the horizon. Companies of the future, and of the present, need to address the issues of their employees, all the issues, and understand that motivation is not always a monetary issue. Certainly people want more money, but the allure of money will not last forever if people are not feeling like they are worthwhile contributors. The workplace must be challenging, yet accepting. There must be independence allowed for folks to do their jobs and yet there must be guidance when needed. Give them the tools to do their job and then stand back and let them do it.

Showing up day after day just for the paycheck weakens motivation. There has to be more. People really do want more.

People Need to Matter

For someone to be truly motivated, they must see that their piece of the puzzle matters. People want to matter. It is a very basic human need. Team leaders need to convey that each individual matters to the whole.

Proper motivation also requires work that fits a person's abilities and desires. Learning what makes people tick is a benefit for the team leader and the members of the team. Sometimes simply rearranging people and their duties makes a world of difference.

Just because a person is in a particular position does not

mean that that person fits that slot. Review the people in your departments or on the project team—who could be a better match doing a different task? Maybe Haley needs to be hunkered down cranking out formulas and algorithms. Haley loves that kind of stuff. Number crunching is exciting for her. Maybe Hank is doing behind-the-scenes stuff but he would be better served, and the team more productive, if he had a more visible role. He excels in communication and delights in conversation with people. Hank should have a position that utilizes his strengths.

What we enjoy and what we are good at, rather than what we are simply assigned, is a whole lot easier to do when time crunch hits and the pressure sets in to meet delivery. If a team member is just doing "some job" that makes him grit his teeth and watch the clock, wishing the day were over, no one is really benefitting. It is hard enough to be in the pressure-cooker situation. The goal is for every teammate to be pulling their fair share and taking pride in what they are doing. Knowing what makes each team member tick is key to knowing what position is a good fit. The best way to accomplish that? Take a little bit of time to talk and get to know them as individuals. It is time well spent in the long run. On every level.

Motivation is a remarkable force. The best workplace (or family or community or relationship) is inspiring and encouraging.

Be Confident, and Inspiring Others Will Be Natural

I believe that everyone has the potential to lead, guide, and motivate others. The confidence to lead is often the missing ingredient, and that is another essential goal of this book. We all need to hear, "Yeah, you did the right thing."

Sometimes we need to hear, "It may be hard, but this is what you have to do." Even when we know what we need to do, that nudge of reassurance can make a world of difference. When you can be true to yourself, you can be true to others.

Be the leader you know you can be.

Maybe it appears that I am painting too rosy a picture. I don't intend to indicate that leadership is a walk in the park or that it's easy. We all know better. Some days, it is easy. It's great. It's wonderful. The pieces fall into place and everyone leaves smiling. But some days, well, let's just say that some days are more difficult than others.

I have talked a lot so far about what to do and what not to do, but let me lay it out there that I am far from perfect. (That goes without saying, of course…just ask my family.) I have what I call my "*Exorcist* moments" when it feels like my head will spin around in a complete 360 and ugly things will come out of me. I get frustrated and there are times when a part of me wants to bang my hands on the table or bite somebody's head off. But really, what does that accomplish? We all have to let off steam in our own way, but doing so on each other reaps absolutely no benefit.

I have learned all along the way, and I am still learning. That is one of the great joys of life, but I also have learned enough to know what works and what doesn't. The knack to work with people comes easily to some. For others, it takes a little time and a little effort to develop the intuition, but it most certainly can be developed. Leadership is a skill, and like all skills, it can be acquired.

One thing all leaders have in common is motivation. They have the drive to succeed, to get it done, and to deliver. They also have the impulse to stir others to action. A good leader is the impetus, but the motivated team is what it takes to maintain the enthusiasm and keep a project on track.

The best leaders have no fear of empathy. Understanding what others are going through is crucial. Empathy is a tool to connect all the members of a team more directly to each other and to a potential solution to problems that they need to solve or a mission they need to accomplish together. "I know what you are going through." "I know what you mean." "I feel your pain."

When different people on the team can see each other as human beings with normal ups and downs, and having some good ideas and some not so good ideas, they can feel for each other. It is not an "each man for himself" kind of mindset. Things get accomplished on an individual level and at the team level. It takes both to achieve delivery and it takes motivation on each team member's part.

The spark to motivate another is in instilling a belief that you can bridge that gap between the now and the soon-to-be. It is, in effect, motivation through understanding. Even if you are not in a position to resolve that challenge for your teammate, you earn respect in the attempt to understand. It's human nature. As a parent, our child may come to us with their first broken heart. There is nothing we can really do about that particular situation, except be there, and let them know that we understand. The common bond of "I know; I get it" goes a long way.

As "the boss," it is very helpful that the team knows that you "get it." That requires being involved at the level where you do in fact understand what is going on and what the hurdles are to overcome. Nothing is more frustrating than a team leader who nods their head in mock empathy, and then turns tail and leaves the team to muck along on their own.

The Second Ingredient: Communicate

This ingredient is a tough one. Communication is an art and everyone does it differently. I've put forward some components of good communication habits, but quite honestly, I could write an entire book on communication and how critical it is to getting things done with a team of people who come from all walks of life and respond to communication in so many different ways.

Remember the exercise earlier in the book? Everyone heard the instructions differently with the paper being folded and ripped. Snowflakes were created, but not consistent results at all. This is why communication is such a key ingredient to your formula for dispelling fear and keeping trollish behavior away.

Communication Is a Tool for Consistent Messaging

The vision for your team, whether you run a department, a company, or a project team, can be seen by all as the same or different depending on your communication style. If you just email everyone the mission, how in goodness' name are they to hear it, feel it and convey it? Think about it. What does "communicate" really mean?

Convey
Impart
Share
Connect
Link
Join

Take a minute to reread that list. Those words are very telling. What is the most important goal of communication? To connect with others. To join together in the same mission or goals. To link the people and the pieces of the delivery puzzle together. It seems pretty obvious, yet we often miss the obvious. In our modern techno world, people still long to connect with other people. We need to help them connect, with leadership, and with each other.

Open Communication Alleviates Fear

Learning to communicate takes time and, like all skills, it is learned by doing. When taking on these new leadership skills, be fearless. It's not just a t-shirt motto. As a leader, you really do need to overcome your inner fears and insecurities. Fake it until you feel the fear and doubts slip away. Remember the commercial tag line, "Never let them see you sweat"? The best way to alleviate fear of the task ahead of you is to share the challenges of the task (not your own fear, but the problem set).

If you communicate openly at all times, the team that works with you knows that you will share the problems at hand and the status of the initiative. When this becomes common practice, and communication is completely open and honest at all times, you will be amazed how your fears about challenges will go by the wayside. Now, everyone is sharing in the challenge and no one is dwelling on what they are afraid of. Too many times, it is not the actual challenge that we fear, but the fear of the unknown, or the fear that others will see that we are not perfect and do not have all the answers.

Don't fool yourself. Being the leader simply means that you will lead, not have super powers.

Communicating Openly Is an Act of Trust

Communication, and its importance, is overlooked because honest, real communication is an act of courage. It takes trust to tell the team what you know—and what you don't know. Being the leader does not mean that you have to be the all mighty and all knowing wizard. No one knows it all and trying to pretend that you do will only alienate those around you. Even that phrase is a derogatory one: Oh, he thinks he's such a "know-it-all." That's not a moniker any one of us wants to be known for.

Even if you know what is going on and it's confidential, I find that telling the team, "Yes, something is going on that requires management thought and decision" helps settle the unrest. I inform them that I will let them know as soon as I know anything. They then stop the massive water cooler talk about "Wow, is something going on?" It gets reduced to "When do you think we will get updated?"

Productivity increases immensely when open and honest communication is a priority. It stops the rumor mill from spiraling out of control and creating negative gossip. The attitude becomes: "If it was really that bad, she wouldn't even let us know it was being talked through."

You're all on the same side. Never lose sight of that.

Having a Conversation Is not Necessarily Communication

Let me say that having a conversation is not the same thing as communication. It's a start. Conversing, even if it's small talk, is a good thing. Getting to know the personalities of those folks that you work with is indeed vital.

Conversations about the weather, the wife, and the weekend are all well and good. Conversation needs to go beyond that and get to the weighty matter of communication. It needs to be an expression of the inner workings of the project and the person and what is needed from each party. To make it all come together, the leader must communicate every day and in every way. Communicate the successes and the progress to spur on more success and progress. A good leader also has to communicate when there is a bottleneck or slowdown or some inevitable hurdle.

As the bumper sticker says, shit happens. Everyone knows it so trying to deny it or sugarcoat it does not win you any points and can in fact be damaging to any trust that you have built up. Yep, back to that issue of trust. It permeates everything.

Learning to trust yourself must occur before you can begin to trust others and before they will be able to trust you. Taking on a leadership role means you have to start trusting yourself.

It's A-OK to Not Know Everything

Know that it's okay to not know everything and know that it's okay that other people also know that you don't know everything. This also goes back to the "no secrets" rule.

I recently had a meeting with the team and the board members of a new project. They were talking about various issues that needed to be addressed and one was a form that needed, or maybe didn't need, to be completed. Discussion went round and round on Form XYZ and I was not familiar with that form. I have been in the banking industry for years, but I didn't know what they were talking about.

I stopped the discussion. "Wait a minute, please. What is Form XYZ? Can I see it? What is it about?"

Were some of the people in the room surprised to learn that I didn't know this form? Maybe. Did it serve any purpose for me to pretend to know what they were talking about? Of course not.

It takes guts to admit that you do not know something. It also creates trust and communication. It shows that everyone is allowed to ask questions and everyone can speak up when they don't know. Trying to fake it will actually impede progress.

Communication Is Fully Dimensional

Actions and words. Mannerisms. Body language. Gestures.

So much of communication is subtle, yet it can scream out so loudly. Arms folded tightly across the chest indicate one message. Hands planted on hips, elbows jutting out, indicate another type of message.

I have been called "Miss Bossy Boots" in jest when I get in my "lay it on the line" mode, but I do not finger-point or pound the table or plant my hands anywhere. I am blunt, but I do everything possible to be respectful.

Everyone needs to be aware of their own body language as well as being tuned in to the language cues of others. What you say and how you say it are equally important. Your unspoken language actually speaks volumes.

Facial expressions carry a lot of weight. Are you prone to rolling your eyes? Work on eliminating that from your silent repertoire. Creating a safe environment for respectful discussion means that your team can trust you to respect them. Rolling the eyes does not indicate a show of respect.

Calm Communication in Less-than-Calm Times Is Critical

You may be frustrated (and be on the brink of having an *Exorcist* moment yourself), but venting in that way (yelling or swearing) at that time serves no purpose. Keeping your cool will win you unspoken points that last forever. They say character is how you behave when no one is looking. It is also how you react when people are watching.

I, too, have struggles with calm communication when I think it's life-threatening if people don't listen, and I work every day to try to improve myself in this regard. There are so many projects I have worked on where many of my colleagues will remember stories of which I am less than proud of my ability to manage calm communication. Each year I get better and now some of the stories have even moved into funny moments, like when my dear friend and colleague was forced to put up with my emotional plea to give us the go-ahead decision on Project Knightsbridge.

A good leader knows when to step in and when to hang back and also when to accept that they weren't perfect and therefore need to enter the next situation improving their approach. Admittedly, some of that intuition may be instinct, but it can also be learned. When your team is equipped properly, they will also be able to come to you when they need guidance or be able to gently remind you that they have the situation under control.

Try Not to Insult Anyone When You Communicate

Maybe your mother told you that if you can't say anything nice, don't say anything at all. That is great advice, but as a leader you are going to have to say something. Watch your words and watch your tone of voice. And watch what your body is saying. When you start paying attention to your own little habits, you might be surprised at what you discover. Being aware is half the battle.

You will want to watch not only how you say what you need to say (which requires common courtesy and empathy), but also be mindful of the little useless "decorations" that often frame the message. For instance, one pet peeve of mine is using, "obviously," or "of course" or "as I already said," in conversation. They have an air of condescension about them that is disruptive and disengaging.

If I say "obviously," maybe it is not obvious to everyone. Or maybe, possibly, I am wrong. Maybe what I think is an obvious solution is actually not. Try not to sprinkle your communication with "obviously," and you won't be stuck making up for it by claiming, "Obviously, I was an idiot." Obviously.

The same goes for "of course." Of course I know all the answers. Of course we should do it my way. Of course I am the big bad boss and you are my underlings hanging on every word I say. Of course I am an idiot. Of course.

Using the phrase "as I have already said" gets old and can be taken as a put down. A lot depends on the tone. As I have already said, my answers are the best. As I have already said, and either you were not listening or too stupid to understand, I will say it again because I am so brilliant and need to say it over and over so you know how brilliant I really am. As I have already said, and I want to pound you over the head with it, I just may be an idiot.

You get my point. Phrases with an air of superiority cause people to tune out what you are saying. All they will be thinking is "Get a load of her. She sure thinks she's something."

Communication Is a Two-Way Street

Communication is a two-way street. You need to edit yourself—words and gestures—to be genuine and welcoming. You need to set the standard for proper communication. In meetings, do not allow disrespect, name-calling or swearing. Be an example and do not tolerate any undermining.

The team needs to know that they can freely communicate their concerns and not be ridiculed or scapegoated or double-crossed. Strong communication is an essential part of a successful team, be it a two-person team or a two hundred-person team.

Communication is an exchange of ideas, not a boss delivering a sermon from on high. It is not a barrel roll of orders or list of the team's failures. It is not about humiliation, but about building up.

The Third Ingredient: Congratulate in More Ways than One

Ah, this is my favorite of the ingredients in your secret formula. I don't like to play favorites and all of the ingredients truly are equal, but this factor gets lost so often in the follow-through. I want to sing the praises of singing praises.

Leaders are just that, someone who leads the rest to the end delivery. The guy in front is not any better than the guy in back; he just is the guy up front. Sometimes it is the guy in front, the "leader," who gets the glory, the kudos, the congrats. A leader without a team is just a guy, standing all alone. One person does not pull off a group project. One person should not get the ovation.

Share the success. Share the spotlight. Share the reward.

Don't save the congratulations for just the finish line. There are many points all along the way where members of the team deserve recognition. Meeting the end delivery only happens because targets are met through each step of the journey. And it is a journey. Complex projects or life together in a family or any kind of relationship is a journey. It is the day in, day out "working it out for the greater good" that gets you across that final finish line.

When I think of congratulations in the workplace, it is more than an "attaboy" and a pat on the back. I don't want to dismiss someone's effort with something that seems dismissive. Does that make sense?

"Attaboys" and "attagirls" are fine, but not enough. I also don't necessarily think that the salary and benefits package is the only means of saying thanks and congrats. I do believe in fair and generous compensation and a host of perks. Bonuses for a job well done can be a great way of saying congratulations. I think that is part of the motivating factor of this equation. Money talks, but so must you.

The money, the bonuses, the mention of a job well done are all-important and I do not discount them one bit. I simply want to remind you that another kind of compensation can be offered—a payment that no accountant can tally on his adding machine, yet one that is immeasurably powerful. I am speaking of a reward of thanks. Gratitude goes a long way.

It needs to be made abundantly clear that the bottom line for job satisfaction is not money. Money is a tempting hold for most folks and it works for a while. People will put up with a lot if they are compensated well. But there comes a point when money is not the panacea.

This principle applies to all aspects of our life. The money earned will become far less important if you don't feel valued. Although no one would usually object to a raise, tossing money at a person is not a viable long-term solution to a dysfunctional, or abusive, situation.

To pass along a genuine "thank you" can stir something in a person. It is empowering and motivating. It is impossible to truly grasp how important it can be. It is the match strike that lights up a person that ignites the candle in their soul.

Praise affirms that you are "doing the right thing," and that you're doing it exceptionally well. Everyone wants and needs to know that they are on the right track. A hearty, sincere "congratulations" feeds the soul. Be lavish with thanks and praise, but be real. False praise is worthless and you lose credibility. Be genuine. Recognize the hard work. Don't be a cheerleader and don't throw empty words around. Keep it real, but when something deserves to be thanked, give it your full gratitude.

It's also extremely valuable to congratulate by ensuring that the management team to which any of your team members report knows how valuable a particular individual has been. Passing on the incredible work that someone has done for you to their next manager goes towards further awards of salary increases but also contributes to the future endeavors that person will be asked to participate in, allowing them to grow in their career.

Since I have discovered that I enjoy acronyms, how about another? Most of the time we think of congratulations at milestone achievement times. Graduations, weddings, etc. What does the graduate wear? A cap and gown. Think CAP:

Congratulate: Make it personal. Reach out to your team individually and as sub-teams and personally let them know how well they have done and how important they were in the project's success. The more personal your congratulations can be, the better. On Project Knightsbridge, we found many ways to congratulate the teams, since many of the teams were responsible for different aspects of the mission, and we wanted to customize the appreciation we felt for them and to show them our true congratulations.

Applaud: Make it public. Everyone must see the great accomplishment and join in on the celebration. Have a real, true celebration and be a part of it. Make it really great and really fun and also introduce some fun awards as part of the public applause!

Praise: Make it match the personal goals of your team. This is your opportunity to put it on the record. Take the initiative throughout the project to understand your team members and their career aspirations. This is your moment to consider their goals and support them through praise. Praise them by ensuring that the next management team they work with knows to call on them and knows what they are made of and how incredible they were to the project's success.

I believe in sharing the success. I believe in sharing the congratulations. I believe it comes back to me and the others on the team when we can applaud each other's efforts and hard work. When one person succeeds, we all succeed. It feels good. Sharing the praise feels good.

Capitalize on the Formula— You Now Have Energy

Encourage the Minds of Your Team

"Empower" and "energy" are not flavor of the month words. I don't want to be trendy. I want to be real. We are all just people, doing our jobs to the best of our abilities. My passion to lead is rooted in my need to be authentic. I don't try to be something I'm not and I don't tell fish tales. If we're in the belly of the whale, I'm going to let my team know and together we will come up with a solution to get us all out of there. Being a leader means that you are always part of the team, an equal part. The part that inspires everyone else to do his or her part. That is my energy and it empowers each person to light up and produce their own energy.

Energy Allows Empowerment to Occur

All the concepts that I talk about in this book are tied together. From the first day that you are in the leadership role, you have to give your whole self, your real self. Remember, there are no secrets and there is no mystery. When communication lines are open and people feel appreciated, trusted, and respected, individuals become empowered. They will trust themselves to do what needs to be done, and if they are in a jam, they know they can ask for help. The atmosphere conducive to empowerment is open, honest, and caring. These are simple, back to basics tactics, nothing tricky, nothing complicated, but not necessarily always easy.

I still like to use the analogy of fireworks. We all have seen fireworks in the night sky at some time in our lives, and many of us still enjoy "oohing" and "ahhing." Fireworks are spectacular. We usually don't think about them; we simply watch and enjoy. The reality is that fireworks are made of several individual ingredients that all come together to create an astonishing piece of work. The results are impressive yet seem so effortless, just needing someone to light the fuse. It is also a very accurate statement that if not handled with care, the fireworks will explode on the ground. That occurrence is rare. Most of the time, we get the fantastic display of everything coming together at just the right time to make something magnificent.

How do you get your team to this point, to the amazing celebration of delivery? Empowerment. Energy. You empower your team, instead of being a powerhouse breathing down over them. It links back to pride. Every employee needs to take ownership of their job, their piece of the puzzle, their square tile on the Rubik's cube. It is your job, the leader's job, to give the tools, the training, the resources and the confidence, if necessary, to allow those team members to take pride in their work.

Authentic Enthusiasm Also Creates Energy

Enthusiasm is a contagion that needs to be spread. And if I show concern with a furrowed brow from time to time, so be it. It goes back to giving one's whole self. Being able to be vulnerable is scary but it is necessary. Your team needs to know that you are there, in every sense of the word: physically, mentally, and emotionally. I want to be authentic, and letting me be me also allows my team to express themselves fully and openly.

I give all of myself to whatever I am dealing with at that moment. I have passion for my job because I love it. I don't do it for the paycheck, although the paycheck is nice. It may sound like a drastic piece of advice, but if you don't love your job, find a way to love it or find a way to leave it. You need to feel passion in what you do, and there is a position out there somewhere that will feed your passion. I honestly believe that.

Build Your Own Toolkit

Your toolkit is yours, all yours. Pack it with the ideas you have learned here and the principles and methods that you know to be true. You have amassed a wealth of knowledge in your life, no matter where you came from, how old you are, or what you do for a living.

Review of the chapters can help you decide what you need to work on and what you feel comfortable with. I think of this toolkit as a program delivery management certification. It is my goal to teach what I know and help others achieve their goals.

This book is a guide, a roadmap of sorts. You take the information presented and make it work for you. You have to customize the tools to work for you in your own style. One of the points mentioned early on was to always be yourself. Put that on a sticky note if you need to.

The toolkit is yours and is ready to take out into what ventures/adventures await. I know the highs and lows, and I also know that the highs are so worth it. I am excited for you!

BACK TO DELIVERY

"We are go for launch" was what was said when Apollo 13 was ready to make its trip into space. On Project Knightsbridge, it felt so similar. I know there were no lives at stake, but there were hundreds of people's careers and pride on the line along with a stock market that could not accept the risk of us making a technical mistake.

"We are a 'go' for implementation," said the two key executives accountable for the legal closing of the merger. My heart was pounding. I knew the team was ready and I had fought so hard with the executives to make this happen, but I was naturally nervous. The technical complexity—not to mention the market exposure if things did not go right—was huge, but off we went to press the first button. The merger integration "GO LIVE" had begun and we had a very tight 60 hours over a long weekend to make it happen.

The first set of milestones had been achieved and it was pretty smooth sailing. At about eighteen hours into the implementation, we were all happy with the results so far. The team was taking turns on breaks and even playing a computer version of King Kong to calm our minds from the stress.

Remember the stress we had around transferring all the assets and the process we would use? Well, it went off without a hitch I was happy that Angie and the SWAT team had worked well and found the right approach. On a comical note, Angie also became the champ in the King Kong game we played at breaks.

At twenty-plus hours into the implementation, our first major problem arose and then a second problem. Remember the two colleagues from the beginning of the book? My mashed potatoes dinner with them? Well, just as we did with any problems that required our attention throughout the project, Lee, Ray and I divided the work when needed and met with the teams facing the trouble issues, and we worked through them. "Always rely on your teammates" is the lesson here. I don't know what I would have done without our constant partnership!

Quiet again, it seemed we might make it to the end without further issues. Then the confirmation came. All milestones were completed and we were early! Everyone went home to get sleep so that when the markets opened the next morning, trading could resume on the new platform. I went back to my hotel. A couple of team members stayed behind just to close up a few things at the office.

I closed my eyes. The phone rang. Houston, we have a problem. It was Marty, my boss. Marty and one other team member, Tim, had stayed at the office to close up. Tim was logging off and noticed a strange message in his queue. He discovered a problem. It appeared that the system we disconnected from the parent company of the old firm was still connected and now the new firm and the old firm could see each other. Oh, my God. How did we miss this? What the hell do we do now? Everyone had gone home to sleep. It was going to be a long night!

Everyone was called back in. Just like with Apollo 13, failure was NOT an option. The team had done everything to get to this day and we were not about to let it go badly now.

The team arrived and it was incredible to watch them overcome the shock and sleepiness, take a deep breath, and find the solution. After five more hours of investigation, Tim and his team discovered that the issue was resolvable and they worked hard to do so. I was so thankful to have Tim on our team. Lee and I had worked hard to recruit him to the team and he had done a fantastic job from day one. So, thankfully the problem was not the disaster it first appeared. You can only imagine our relief! It really was done! Back to sleep everyone went!

Chapter 7

The Mountain Has Moved

WE NOW KNOW "HOW" TO DELIVER. All five steps have been completed and the mountain has moved. Wow. Exhale. It's due to your ability to take your knowledge of the "what" and put the "how" in action. Now it is time to reflect on what has truly been achieved, appreciate the success and then move on to the next challenge!

> 1. **You Have Embraced the Challenge**
> 2. **You Have Formed a Winning Team**
> 3. **You Are the Leader**
> 4. **You Have Healthy Soft Skills**
> 5. **You Made It Happen**

Although this is not the typical "how-to" management book, I do explain the "how," and you can apply these simple concepts to wherever you are in life. The information gleaned from these chapters can assist you in "managing" all areas of your life. I don't want to get hung up on terms, because this is not a "business babble" book; this book is for everyone, regardless of vocation, position, or career. I talk about business situations because that is my area of expertise, but the concepts are applicable to whatever is going on in your life.

I may be known as a leader, but I believe that everyone has the potential to lead, guide, and motivate others. The confidence to lead is often the missing ingredient, and that is another essential goal of this book. When you are faced with a new situation, a presentation, an interview, or a complex project, you can refer back to the chapters here to renew your belief in your own abilities. When you need a dose of encouragement, words from a friend, I hope this book can fill that need if your friend doesn't pick up the phone. Remember, we all need to hear, "Yeah, you did the right thing." Sometimes we need to hear, "It may be hard, but this is what you gotta do." Even when we know what we need to do, that nudge of reassurance can make a world of difference. When you can be true to yourself, you can be true to others.

It is also my wish that when you are done with this book, just seeing it on your bookshelf will be a reminder of the power within you and the power within those around you, and how that power is magnified exponentially when you pool your powers. (That's kind of catchy. Maybe "Pool Your Powers" should have been considered for a book title.)

It is my sincere hope that my experiences, the tales from the trenches, the idea of peopledemia, and the notion that results can be delivered despite all odds will inspire you to be a leader—in your workplace, in your home, and in your community. To be a successful leader, someone who gets the job done and knows how to lead others effectively, is my goal for my life and for this book. "How to get anything done no matter how difficult it may seem" is a great subtitle.

SUCCESS MUST BE CELEBRATED

The team's success is a moment to thank them again, and to be grateful for all that they have done. Each team member should know that their own personal contribution has been noticed and appreciated. The management should show its appreciation to the team for raising the company's profile and completing the mission with an outstanding result.

One of the wonderful benefits of working with a team of people that you admire is that all of their individual qualities reflect on the company or organization as a whole. The sum is greater than its parts. I could not have done my job on Project Knightsbridge without the teammates I worked with and so many of them deserved to be named in more stories, but there just wasn't the room in this book.

A group of unique and separate individuals meshed into a productive, efficient, and trustworthy team. A new level of respect was created all around. You will miss your team when you move on to your next challenge. I know I miss my teammates every time!

A NEW CULTURE IS BORN

After months of intense work and forming relationships, my part comes to an end. I am hired to pull off projects and that is what I do. Wait. That is what WE do. The high-performing team is the bottom line. Over the course of a project, we form a bond and share the thrill of project completion and project success. We are all better off from the lessons we have learned about hard work and the joy of a job well done.

When delivery occurs, my job is over. I move on to the next project in crisis and apply these same principles to a new team and a new set of goals needing to be delivered. I have learned that the five steps work. The team members have learned that as well.

Prior to joining this team and this project, some team members may have experienced poor circumstances in past jobs or with past managers. This new knowledge base and toolkit is the opportunity to spread the wealth to future teams and projects.

I always meet with the team before I move on to other things so that we can talk and be reminded of what they have achieved and that it is so much more than the work mission accomplished. The delivery is the key, but how we were able to achieve that delivery is what they need to take with them (the what and the how!). They have achieved a way of working that rises above competition and corporate ladder climbing.

Each team member should now be able to leave this project

and move on to other ventures, left with a new culture to pay it forward. The experience of working with a great leader affects the team and energizes them in their future endeavors. Great leaders create more great leaders. The sign of a great leader is the ability, and the desire, to move mountains without crushing the villagers.

I hope by now that you understand, really get, that people matter. I also hope that you understand this book as more than one more business book or another project management manual and take to heart the message.

My motivation for writing this book was to open minds to a needed shift in mindset, a new way of thinking. What we think controls how we act. First the mind, then actions and attitudes follow.

I have to say it one more time. People matter.

YOUR TOOLKIT AND DELIVERY SUCCESSES

I have repeated my mantra in the earlier chapters, stressing the concept that people matter. Yes, that is true, most definitely, but it's more than that. It's about taking what you know in your head and applying it to your daily behavior. It is also customizing your approach as you learn from others additional great ways to make things happen, while holding the priorities of people dear to you.

You now know that a successful leader understands that each person has a separate code or combination, like a lock. Your toolkit, your bag of leadership skills, needs to be able to crack each person's code. Some leaders take a stick of dynamite and try to force their way in. Others only know how to relate to a person who ticks in a similar way that they do. Those locks might be easier to decode, but there is a whole company full of people to reach.

An effective leader has to care enough to figure out the combination of the members of his or her team. The skilled leader has to invest the time to learn how each person is wired. What cracks the code for one will not crack the code for all. You will also need to find the code to crack for your own lock to improve your own abilities. We are not perfect leaders, but we must be committed leaders.

With all the different tools in your toolkit, you have to sift through it and make it work for you. Take the pearls of wisdom that speak to you. Let the others ruminate in the back of your mind. Maybe some day they will work for you, too. Life is all about learning, growing and improving.

Let's stop and remember what is in our toolkit so far:

1. **Embrace the Challenge Using the 3 Cs**
2. **Form the Winning Team With DEUCES**
3. **Be the Leader by Mastering the Art of Leadership**
4. **Stock up on the Soft Skills With the 4 Ls**
5. **Make It Happen With a Secret Formula**

The five steps and the five tools within your toolkit all join to make delivery easier and leadership more positive. Leadership is also about helping and sharing. As you become a leader in your area, large or small or something in between, share what you know. Help others learn how to deal with the dynamics of people. Teach them what you know and what works for you. When you share, you also learn. A person who stops learning is a person who has stopped breathing.

We all have something to contribute and we can all do our part to move the mountain. The real trick is keeping people and the village intact as we go about the process. Life is full of challenges. Learning how to deal with stress and be the calming influence will serve you well in any situation. When you are congratulated for your success and someone asks you, "How do you do it?" I hope you will take the time to tell them. Let's all keep paying it forward.

IT'S A WRAP!

We're all human and the dynamics of our interactions are what make the world go 'round and what makes or breaks a project. That's the real bottom line. As for the London merger, the first day, the second day and into the fifth day of trading went well. We could now celebrate—and, believe me, we did.

After an intense ninety-seven days, it was time to say goodbye.

Two weeks before Project Knightsbridge wrapped, a colleague in the States had called and asked if there was anything that we needed or wanted.

"Rold Gold pretzels," I replied. "We're out and we can't get them here." Then I forgot about that phone call while we were in the last stages before the "go live" date.

Day ninety-seven arrived and we had pulled it off! Project Knightsbridge had been a tricky one, to say the very least, and it was a major feat. We celebrated in a big way. A big way. The next day, hangover day, we were packing up the office, exhausted but proud and happy. A shipment arrived—a large crate of Rold Gold pretzels.

This was no ordinary box. This was a pallet of pretzels, a five-foot by four-foot by four-foot carton of salty snacks. It was big, just like what we had gone through. The accomplishment was big; the success was big. I felt validated. We all did. I was so proud of everyone.

In the end, my newness to the company and the team had never hindered the project. Applying everything I knew and everything that I believed in about human nature and teamwork proved that people could work together in extreme conditions and still come through the other side with self-respect, respect for each other, and that incredible, proud, happy, tingly feeling inside that we did it together.

My job there was done. I had said my goodbyes. I opened the gigantic box, took a bag of pretzels, and got on the plane for home.

Author's Note

So many people were involved with Project Knightsbridge and should be personally mentioned in this book, but space does not permit. There were the individuals you've read about throughout the book like Lee and Ray, but there were so many others I wish I could acknowledge.

I thank all of them and would like to make a special mention to those who went on to face the challenges of 9/11, including a thoughtful dedication to a gentleman by the name of Rich Lee ("Tim" in the Project Knightsbridge story) who we lost when the twin towers went down that fateful day, September 11th, 2001.

The Project Knightsbridge team is one of many teams that I have been honored to work with, and I thank all of the other teams that have come before and since – they all have taught me "It's all in the delivery."

For further information, please visit:
www.Itsallinthedelivery.ca